Laurie Cole | Emily E. Ryan

glo

365 Devotions
to Give God *Priority*

Compilation • Emily E. Ryan
Production / Interior Layout • Pam Henderson
Cover Design / Interior Design • Jason Ryan

Priority Ministries
Encouraging Women to Give God Glory & Priority

www.priorityministries.com

´glō: to give God glory

Since 2004, Priority Ministries has encouraged
and equipped over 50,000 women and teens
to give God glory and priority in their everyday lives.

Whether you've been with us from the beginning
or you're discovering us for the first time,
this book is dedicated to you.

May you grow and *glo* as you love Him most
and seek Him first.

Laurie Cole

Emily E. Ryan

About the Authors

Laurie Cole is the founder and President of Priority Ministries and has been a speaker at women's events and conferences throughout the country for over 25 years.

Laurie first developed a passion for in-depth Bible study as a Precepts student and is now the author of five Bible studies for women, including *There is a Season: Experiencing Contentment in Every Season of Life*, *Beauty by The Book: Becoming a Biblically Beautiful Woman*, and *Are You a Disciple? Saying YES to a Life Beyond Casual Christianity* (available 2015). Her studies have reached over 50,000 women in homes and churches in the U.S., Canada and overseas.

Laurie and her husband, Bill, serve the Lord at Sagemont Church in Houston, Texas where he is the Associate Pastor of Worship & Praise. They've been blessed with three fantastic sons (David, Kevin, and J.J.), two wonderful daughters-in-law (Stephanie and Rachael), and three glorious grandchildren (Ezra, Juliette and Caroline).

Facebook:	facebook.com/lauriecole.priorityministries
Twitter:	twitter.com/LaurieMCole

Emily E. Ryan is a Christian women's author and speaker and serves as the Executive Editor of Priority Ministries.

A writer since the age of ten, Emily's books naturally reflect her own insights and experiences with the universal struggles that plague the hearts of many Christian women. Her most recent book, *Guilt-Free Quiet Times: Exposing the Top Ten Myths about Your Time with God*, flowed from the desperate need to rebuke perfectionism, reclaim grace and rediscover the joy of spending time with God, and her first book, *Who Has Your Heart? The Single Woman's Pursuit of Godliness*, was born out the tension that exists between the desire to be married and the desire to submit to God's timing for marriage.

She and her husband, Jason, live outside of Houston, Texas, and attend Sagemont Church where he serves as the Music and Communications Director. They have four young children who love to thank God for Minecraft, Skylanders, Elsa and Mickey Mouse.

When she's not writing, she can sometimes be found pushing a stroller around her neighborhood while riding her unicycle.

Facebook:	facebook.com/emilyeryan.writer
Twitter:	twitter.com/writeremilyryan

*To inquire about having Laurie or Emily speak at your event,
to preview our resources, or to support Priority with your
financial gift, visit us online at priorityministries.com*

Contents

january

January 1

Finish strong

Now finish the work, so that your eager willingness to do it may be matched by your completion of it, according to your means.
2 Corinthians 8:11 NIV

Starting is a whole lot easier than finishing. That truth remains whether you're starting a devotional book, a diet, a marriage, a degree, a scrapbook, a race, or a million other things. It's just plain hard to finish, much less to finish strong.

January 1st usually isn't a day that people think about finishing. Instead they focus on starting. But the potential of a new year, the excitement of new goals, and all the things that work to catapult you from the starting point are all but forgotten at the finish line.

Whatever spiritual goals you have set for yourself this year, it is important to know ahead of time that finishing will be difficult. Your enthusiasm and stamina will fade, you will grow weary, and you may question if it's even worth it. So before you even start, pray for the strength to finish strong. God will help you. You *can* do it, and it is worth it.

Emily

Show me Your list

Show me your ways, Lord, teach me your paths.
Psalm 25:4 NIV

Hyper list-making mode. That pretty much describes the first week of January for list-makers like me.

I have lists of personal goals, family goals, ministry and work goals, household projects for me, and honey-dos for my husband. Need a list? I can make you one! Girl, January 1st kicks list-makers like me into overdrive.

But even if you love lists like I do, sometimes they can hurt more than help.

- Instead of helping us organize, they overwhelm.
- Instead of helping us clarify, they clutter.
- Instead of helping us analyze, they paralyze.

This January, don't make one single goal, resolution, or list, without first praying, "Lord, show me Your list—Your goals and Your vision—for my life this year."

Laurie

GloFish

You are the light of the world.
Matthew 5:14 NIV

"GloFish" are fluorescent fish that appear to glow both in everyday light and even more so under black lights (www.GloFish.com). Originally bred to help detect environmental pollutants, anyone can now purchase these unique fish for his or her own personal aquarium. The amazing thing about these fish is that they are not dyed or painted. They have actually been genetically enhanced with a fluorescent protein gene so that they "glow" from the inside!

When Christ is in you, it's His light (or the supernatural fluorescent Christ gene, if you will) that glows within you. To truly *glo*, or glorify Him, is to *glo* from the inside!

Emily

Your foundation

*Anyone who listens to my teaching and follows it is wise, like a person
who builds a house on solid rock. Though the rain comes in torrents
and the floodwaters rise and the winds beat against that house,
it won't collapse because it is built on bedrock.*
Matthew 7:24-25 NLT

You can know God's way for your life when you know His
Word. His Word needs to be the foundation of your life.
You need to give it priority. You must know what you believe, and
your beliefs must be based on the truth of God's Word. Only then
can you keep from falling when the winds and rains come.

In this world of politically correct ideals, there are constantly
changing values in our culture. What was right yesterday is wrong
today. What was wrong yesterday is right today. You can't just
put your finger up to test the direction of the wind, take a poll
or Google your values for the day. You need to *know* what you
believe and then you can make your decisions based on truth.

Laurie

A gentle whisper

*After the earthquake came a fire, but the Lord was not in the fire.
And after the fire came a gentle whisper. When Elijah heard it,
he pulled his cloak over his face and went out and stood
at the mouth of the cave.*
1 Kings 19:12-13 NIV

The Lord told Elijah to go and stand on the mountain because He was about to pass by (1 Kings 19:11-13). Elijah watched as a great wind came and shattered the rocks. Then a great earthquake shook the ground followed by a mighty blazing fire. But God was in none of these. Finally came a gentle whisper. It was the whisper of the Lord.

Writer Michael Hyatt calls this world a "noisy" world. That couldn't be more true. It's loud. It's big. It's full of screaming advertisements and loud, constant chaos that demands your attention every single moment. But not only does it demand your attention; it also demands your response. Do you listen? Do you follow? Do you get distracted by the glitz and the razzle dazzle? Or do you ignore the screams and instead tune in to the gentle whisper of the Lord?

God is a gentleman. He doesn't shout His commands like a drill sergeant or have a tantrum like a two-year-old. He speaks carefully, quietly, and intentionally into your heart through His Holy Spirit.

Can you hear Him? Are you listening?

Emily

A crisis of faith

Consider it all joy, my brethren, when you encounter various trials,
knowing that the testing of your faith produces endurance.
And let endurance have its perfect result, so that you
may be perfect and complete, lacking in nothing.
James 1:2-4 NASB

What you believe is going to be put to the test, so don't be surprised. Sometimes we feel guilty because we have these big questions or doubts about God. We ask, "God, how could you do this to me?" and we begin to think things we never thought we'd think before about the God we love so much. When a crisis comes, sometimes we're so traumatized that we can't even think straight.

Don't worry, doubt, or feel guilty about uncertainty that comes when you're in a crisis. There will be times when your faith is going to be tested, and those feelings are completely normal. In fact, it's the very process of moving forward *with* your uncertainty that causes your faith to grow stronger.

Laurie

Start with milk

I gave you milk, not solid food, for you were not yet ready for it.
Indeed, you are still not ready.
1 Corinthians 3:2 NIV

The Bible refers to us as infants when we are early on in our spiritual growth, and we have to grow in Christ just like we grow physically. But not all aspects of your walk with Christ will grow at the same speed. You may be mature in prayer, but immature in your knowledge of the Bible; you may be mature in faith, but immature in your giving.

Consider if there are any areas of your spiritual life where you're still in the infant stage. Since the wisdom of spiritual growth lies in starting as a child and growing to maturity, there's no reason why those areas can't be approached with the same advice. You can start small. You *can* start with milk! If you've never read your Bible, you can start by reading just a few verses a day. If you've never tithed to your church, you can start with just a few dollars a week.

Your desire may be for solid food. You may want to be as spiritually mature as your pastor or teacher is right now. But for today, start with milk. You'll mature to solid food in time.

Emily

Dry spell

For God has said, "I will never fail you. I will never abandon you."
So we can say with confidence, "The Lord is my helper,
so I will have no fear."
Hebrews 13:5-6 NLT

Perhaps you are experiencing a dry season in your spiritual life. Sometimes we may feel God is distant because we cannot seem to connect with Him even when we pray and even when we know there is no personal sin blocking our fellowship with Him. In truth, however, seasons change but God does not. He promises that He will never leave you and He will always be your helper.

If you are experiencing a spiritual "dry spell," use God's Word to cry out to Him. "My soul cleaves to the dust; Revive me according to Your word" (Ps. 119:25 NKJV). By faith, believe He hears. By faith, believe He will soon answer and revive you.

Laurie

Discernment in action

*Now the Bereans were of more noble character than
the Thessalonians, for they received the message with great
eagerness and examined the Scriptures every day to see
if what Paul said was true.*

Acts 17:11 NIV

The prompting of the Holy Spirit is not to be ignored.
The book of Acts tells of the Bereans who sat under the
teachings of Paul. Every day they took what they heard from Paul
and tested it against the Scriptures to see if his message was true
or not, and they were commended for their discernment.

What about you? Do you examine the preachers you hear or the
books you read against the Bible? Or do you just take everything at
face value and assume it's accurate without examining it yourself?
God gave us the ultimate authority (the Bible) for a reason.
Read it. Study it. And test everything according to it. Over time,
you will become more sensitive to the truth and half-truths
around you, and your sense of discernment will be heightened.

Emily

The immature and irresponsible

Encourage those who are timid. Take tender care of those who are weak. Be patient with everyone.
I Thessalonians 5:14 NLT

When you are among people who are immature and irresponsible in their faith, there are several things you can do to help them. First, you should encourage them. Avoid taking them to task all the time and pointing out only the things that they are doing wrong. Instead find the areas where they are doing well and encourage them in those.

Secondly, you are to help or support them. Maybe they've fallen. Be the one to help them up and then prop them up to keep them from falling again. Help them make wise decisions. Reassure them that you will not give up on them.

Lastly, you should be patient. Remember that we have all been immature and irresponsible before. We've needed the encouragement, help and patience of the Holy Spirit and they deserve nothing less.

Laurie

January 11

Let us go right into the presence of God with sincere hearts fully trusting him. For our guilty consciences have been sprinkled with Christ's blood to make us clean, and our bodies have been washed with pure water.
Hebrews 10:22 NIV

Only the blood of Christ can make us truly clean. His blood covers our sins and washes away our iniquities. But it's important to consider that the blood of Christ works more like bleach than like soap. If I wash a piece of fabric with soap, I may be able to remove the stains and make it appear clean from the outside. But, if I bleach the fabric, I can change the inside as well as the outside. The bleach soaks into every nook and cranny of the material and changes the color of each individual fiber.

Emily

Face to face

*And let us not neglect our meeting together, as some people do,
but encourage one another, especially now that the day of
his return is drawing near.*
Hebrews 10:25 NLT

In today's digital world, it's easy to forget the importance of face-to-face meetings. Emails, social media, text messages and note cards are good, but they're not always enough. They don't replace the comfort, encouragement and joy you receive from seeing someone in person.

Is there someone who could benefit from seeing you face-to-face? Is there someone you need to see in person to lift your spirits? You may need to go to church, join a small group, or just plan a lunch date with a friend. But whatever it takes to increase the time you spend with your loved ones, do it. You will both benefit from the face time.

Emily

January 13

What next?

*Then Naomi said to her two daughters-in-law,
"Go back, each of you, to your mother's home.
May the Lord show you kindness, as you have shown
kindness to your dead husbands and to me."*
Ruth 1:8 NIV

In the beginning of the book of Ruth, we see three women in crisis each come to a fork in the road. After losing their husbands, Naomi and her daughters-in-law, Ruth and Orpah, had to decide, "What next?" Naomi was spiritually empty, but she held on to the small sliver of faith that she had left and let that lead her back to Bethlehem and back to the Lord. Orpah had great intentions, but ultimately returned to the life that was comfortable and normal for her. Ruth had no idea what a future in Bethlehem would look like, so she paved her steps with the promises of the Lord.

Over your life, you will be faced with many choices, you will come to many forks in the road and your faith will be revealed by the choices you make.

Laurie

First steps

*When Naomi heard in Moab that the Lord had come to
the aid of his people by providing food for them, she and her
daughters-in-law prepared to return home from there.*
Ruth 1:6 NIV

The road to God's new beginning starts with a simple and perhaps a wobbly baby step of faith. That's what Naomi did in the book of Ruth. She got up one morning and she summoned all the courage she had and all the faith she had, even though it was very little, and she said, "I'm going to take a baby step of faith. I'm determined to live, and I'm going to go forward."

That's when the road to a new beginning begins for you and me too, with that scary, wobbly, unsteady first step of faith.

Laurie

Empty

> She said to them, "Do not call me Naomi; call me Mara,
> for the Almighty has dealt very bitterly with me. I went out full,
> but the Lord has brought me back empty. Why do you call me
> Naomi, since the Lord has witnessed against me and
> the Almighty has afflicted me?"
> Ruth 1:20-21 NASB

You may connect with Naomi's words. You may feel as though God has dealt bitterly with you and has brought you to an empty place. You wonder, "God are you against me? What have I done wrong? God, I was a good worker. I don't deserve a pink slip. I was a good wife. I don't deserve for him to have an affair. I was a good mother, but my children have broken my heart. What is going on? You must have turned your back on me."

That's exactly how Naomi felt as she walked away from Moab towards Bethlehem bereft of her husband and sons. She believed that God had dealt bitterly with her and she didn't like what God had done one bit. What she couldn't see, however, was how God was working behind the scenes.

Laurie

A new beginning

So Naomi returned, and with her Ruth the Moabitess,
her daughter-in-law, who returned from the land of Moab.
And they came to Bethlehem at the beginning of barley harvest.
Ruth 1:22 NASB

There was something that Naomi and Ruth did not realize as they walked away from Moab towards Bethlehem. They did not realize that it was the beginning of a harvest. They were desperate and alone. They were discouraged and afraid, and every dream that they dreamed had been shattered. But what they saw as the end of hope was really a new beginning in disguise.

I don't know what desperate situation you are facing right now. It may feel like the end, and you may barely have a shred of faith to hold onto. But I want you to hang on to that shred of faith and know that God is going to bless you and that He is going to give you, in His time, a new beginning.

Laurie

January 17

Happened to come

*So she departed and went and gleaned in the field after the reapers;
and she happened to come to the portion of the field belonging to
Boaz, who was of the family of Elimelech.*
Ruth 2:3 NASB

When we read that Ruth "happened to come" to the field of Boaz, the very man who would become her husband and kinsman-redeemer, it reads like a lucky coincidence. Like Ruth just happened to be at the right place at the right time.

Nothing could be further from the truth. The truth is that because Ruth was walking obediently by faith, God was able to direct her steps and sovereignly put her in the right field. He led Ruth's feet to Boaz's field that day. He arranged and orchestrated her divine encounter so smoothly that on the surface it looks like a coincidence. And He will do for us what He did for Ruth. If we allow Him to direct our steps, He will direct us to be at the right place at the right time.

Laurie

Honor your parents

Honor your father and mother, as the Lord your God commanded you.
Deuteronomy 5:16 NLT

"Honor your father and mother" is the first "horizontal" commandment given in the Ten Commandments. It's important. There is a reason why you have the parents that you have. God chose the exact time and place where you would live and the exact family into which you would be born or adopted. By respecting and honoring the people God chose to be your parents, you are respecting God's decision to place you under their authority.

Honoring your parents does not end when you become an adult, and it doesn't end when your parents pass away. It is an unconditional commandment that has no expiration date. You do not have to agree with them in order to honor them, but you do have to respect their position in your life.

Emily

On your mark

*Let us run with endurance the race God has set before us.
We do this by keeping our eyes on Jesus, the champion who
initiates and perfects our faith. Because of the joy awaiting him,
he endured the cross, disregarding its shame.*
Hebrews 12:1-2 NLT

On your mark, get set, GO! That's what most days feel like—the start of a race. A race to accomplish everything on your to-do list at home. A race to complete everything on your to-do list at work. A race to plan meals, buy groceries, prepare meals, and clean up after meals. A race to run errands, fight the traffic and deal with all of those other drivers, too.

It's a new day and the race is on. But focusing on your to-do list, getting things done, or consuming massive amounts of vitamins and caffeine won't help you cross the finish line God's way. The only way to run the race and finish well is by keeping your eyes on Jesus. So, focus on Him and follow His example today and you'll find all of the strength and inspiration you need to run. And run. And run.

On your mark, get set, *GLO!*

Laurie

I'll pray for you

*Carry each other's burdens, and in this way
you will fulfill the law of Christ.*
Galatians 6:2 NIV

Have you ever found yourself telling someone, "I'll pray for you," knowing full well that you probably won't? Sometimes you'd rather "do" instead of pray, and sometimes, you just plain forget. But carrying each other's burdens via prayer is not a suggestion; it's a command.

I am always encouraged to pray for others when I read Paul's letters. When he writes to the people in various churches he visited, he often mentions that he is praying for those he met. He is genuinely concerned about their spiritual growth and prays for them with prayers that address their current situations.

Consider committing these four passages to memory or writing them on note cards that you can keep in your wallet. Next time you tell someone that you'll pray for her, use one of Paul's prayers as a guideline: Eph. 3:16-19, Phil. 1:9-11, Col. 1:9-12, and 2 Thess. 1:11-12.

Emily

January 21

Everywhere

Where can I go from your Spirit?
Where can I flee from your presence?
Psalm 139:7 NIV

There is nowhere you can go that is out of reach for God. He does not communicate with you based on real estate. He wants to meet with you regardless of where you are.

Are you in the hospital? God is there. Are you in a teacher's lounge? God is there. Are you in your car? In the shower? On the subway? On a ski lift? In your laundry room? In prison? Waiting in line? On an airplane? At the gym? At a bar? On the mission field? In your garden?

God goes to all of those places too.

Emily

He holds your hand

*The LORD directs the steps of the godly. He delights in
every detail of their lives. Though they stumble, they will never fall,
for the LORD holds them by the hand.*
Psalm 37:23-24 NLT

A new day stretches out before you today. A new day filled with:

Blessings and challenges.
Ups and downs.
Questions and answers.
Laughter and tears.

In every high and every low, may His words bring you comfort, confidence, and the calm assurance of His companionship:

God directs your steps.
God delights in every detail of your life.
God holds your hand. Even when you stumble. He will not let you fall.
Rest in His promises.
Recognize His divine presence.

And remember, He holds your hand.

Laurie

January 23

Are you missing something?

I will study your commandments and reflect on your ways.
Psalm 119:15 NLT

Are you counting on preachers, teachers and writers for all of your biblical knowledge? If so, you will miss something. Not everything gets taught on Sunday mornings. Not every passage in the Bible makes it onto the best-sellers lists. There are many hidden nuggets of truth tucked away in the Bible that you will discover only from reading it on your own.

When preachers and teachers talk, it's often on a general, broad level, trying to reach the most people possible in the short amount of time that they have. Books can sometimes go deeper and supplement your time with the Lord, but they are not meant to replace it. Study His commandments on your own. Reflect on His ways. Feel free to use other materials for help, but be careful not to neglect one-on-one time with God's Word.

Emily

The flesh

*So then, on the one hand I myself with my mind am serving the
law of God, but on the other, with my flesh the law of sin.*
Romans 7:25 NASB

The sinful nature, or the flesh, is the root problem of the
ongoing war we experience in our Christian walk. Does this
mean that our physical flesh is our problem and our enemy? No.
The Bible Knowledge Commentary says that the sinful nature,
or flesh, does not refer to "literal physical or material flesh, but
(to) the principle of sin that expresses itself through one's mind
and body."[1]

The Greek word for sinful nature, or flesh, is *sarx* which means
"sinfulness, proneness to sin, the carnal nature, the seat of carnal
appetites and desires, of sinful passions and affections whether
physical or moral."[2]

Upon salvation we receive a new nature through the indwelling of
the Holy Spirit. The old sinful nature, however, is not eradicated at
salvation. Therefore, these two natures are at war within the life
of every believer. The old nature, which produces the desire to
walk in sinfulness, is at war with the new nature, which produces
the desire to walk in righteousness. Praise God that "there
is now no condemnation for those who are in Christ Jesus"
(Rom. 8:1 NASB).

Laurie

Undignified

David, wearing a linen ephod, danced before the LORD with all his might, while he and the entire house of Israel brought up the ark of the LORD with shouts and the sound of trumpets.
2 Samuel 6:14-15 NIV

David knew the significance of bringing the Ark of the Covenant back to Jerusalem. The Ark was synonymous with God's presence. With His will. With His protection and His blessing over the nation of Israel. By celebrating the return of the Ark, he was celebrating Israel's relationship with God. To jump and shout and sing and dance with no inhibitions and no qualms about propriety was simply a natural response to the supernatural influence of the Lord upon his heart.

And so he celebrated. With all his might.

Do you celebrate the Lord like David did? Or does a bowl game in overtime get you more fired up? Or your child's dance recital? Or your compensation plan? Or your engagement? Your retirement? Your remission? Your grandchildren? God allows us to enjoy many things, but do we enjoy *Him*?

I will probably never shave my head for Vacation Bible School or paint my face pink to celebrate the spiritual growth in my Bible study class, but I pray that, like David, "I will celebrate before the Lord." And, maybe, just maybe, "I will become even more undignified than this" (2 Sam. 6:21-22 NIV).

Emily

Prodigals

*Jesus continued: "There was a man who had two sons. The younger
one said to his father, 'Father, give me my share of the estate.'
So he divided his property between them. Not long after that, the
younger son got together all he had, set off for a distant country
and there squandered his wealth in wild living."*
Luke 15:11-13 NIV

We're all at risk of being prodigals like the Prodigal Son.
There is something tantalizing about going outside the will
of God The thrill of the forbidden. The draw of an easier, more
exciting, or greener path than the one that you're on right now.
We've all been tempted to go outside the will of God for some
reason or another.

The question is, are you aware of what draws you away from the
path He's laid out for you? Are you trying to rush His timing?
Are you considering taking a short cut through a difficult situation,
even if it means being somewhere you shouldn't be? Or are you
enjoying your comfort zone so much that you're not willing to
forfeit your feelings of security?

Emily

January 27

Dealing with worry

Who of you by worrying can add a single hour to your life?
Luke 12:25 NIV

Are you worried? If so, you may be on the right track by voicing your concerns to God through prayer. But if you're walking away from those prayers still feeling stress instead of peace, then you're not just concerned; you're worried. And worry, my friend, is sin.

The way to deal with worry is to first call it what it is. Worry is faithlessness and faithlessness is a sin. Second, you must deal with worry like you deal with all sin and confess it (1 John 1:9). Last, you must follow Peter's words in 1 Peter 5:7 and cast it away. "Cast all your anxiety on him because he cares for you" (NIV).

Call it. Confess it. Cast it. Conquer your worry before it conquers you.

Laurie

Set it shine

*You are the light of the world. A city on a hill cannot be hidden.
Neither do people light a lamp and put it under a bowl. Instead
they put it on its stand, and it gives light to everyone in the house.
In the same way, let your light shine before men, that they may
see your good deeds and praise your Father in heaven.*
Matthew 5:14-16 NIV

We live in a dark and fallen world. Like a storm that casts a shadow of darkness along its path, sin covers our eyes and blinds us from the face of God. But, if we are in Christ, we have become the light of the world because we have received the source of the light: Jesus.

Sometimes our relationship with Christ is such that our light shines like a spotlight onto the hearts of those around us, but other times, we are less confident in sharing our faith. It helps to remember that even the dimmest of lights, like the faint glow of a cell phone, can provide relief to a world bathed in darkness. We are commanded by Christ to be the light of the world and to share His truth with others, and that command is not dependent upon the strength of our relationship or the brightness of our lights. For our world is so dark and so blind that its eyes ache for a glimmer of light revealing even the slightest glimpse of the Lord. Be that light to someone today.

Emily

Dwelling

The Word became flesh and made his dwelling among us.
We have seen his glory, the glory of the one and only Son,
who came from the Father, full of grace and truth.
John 1:14 NIV

The word "dwelling" in John 1:14 is especially significant for us. In the Greek, this word means "to encamp, pitch a tent... to dwell as in tents, to tabernacle."[3] Through this word, we see the beauty and symbolism of the Old Testament tabernacle as it foreshadowed Christ who came to earth, pitched His tent and "tabernacled" among men.

Isn't it amazing that Christ left the courts of heaven to dwell among sinful men, enabling them not only to witness but also to partake in His glory!

Laurie

Questioning God

*Then Job replied to the Lord: "I know that you can do anything, and
no one can stop you. You asked, 'Who is this that questions my
wisdom with such ignorance?' It is I—and I was talking about
things I knew nothing about, things far too wonderful for me."*
Job 42:1-3 NIV

How many times do we continue to question God just like
Job did and naively expect that He will answer us according
to our own satisfaction? We imagine that He'll give us perfect
insight into His divine ways every time, and we forget that there
are some times that things will always remain a little blurry.
God is God and His ways are higher than our ways. Sometimes
He will grant us clarity and perfect vision, and other times He
will just keep His ways a mystery. He does not owe us an
explanation, nor does He owe us perfect vision, even in hindsight.
He is, after all, God. And we are not.

Emily

Etcetera

> *Whether you turn to the right or to the left, your ears will hear a*
> *voice behind you, saying, "This is the way; walk in it."*
> Isaiah 30:21 NIV

Have you ever wished that there was a book of Etcetera in the Bible? Something straight from God with clear answers to all of those gray-area questions like: How many children should we have? When should I retire? Which major should I choose? Should we go with logo A or logo B for our new business? Whom should I marry?

God didn't give us the book of Etcetera because it would have ruined our relationship with Him. If you had an Etcetera-kind of book of the Bible, you'd be more likely to treat God like a Magic 8 Ball, running to Him whenever you have a question and forgetting about Him two seconds after you have your answer. But God wants to be more to you than that. He wants you to know Him intimately, to trust Him completely and to depend on Him entirely.

The answers to those gray-area questions become clearer the closer you are to God. Sure, they're never as black-and-white as a "Thou shalt" or "Thou shalt not" command, but as your relationship with Him grows over time, it becomes easier to know His will when things aren't as easy as black and white.

Emily

february

Names the stars

Lift up your eyes and look to the heavens: Who created all these?
He who brings out the starry host one by one and calls forth each of
them by name. Because of his great power and mighty strength,
not one of them is missing.
Isaiah 40:26 NIV

On February 1, 2003, President George W. Bush responded to the Space Shuttle Columbia tragedy with these words from Isaiah 40. Here is what he said:

In the skies today we saw destruction and tragedy. Yet farther than we can see, there is comfort and hope. In the words of the prophet Isaiah, "Lift your eyes and look to the heavens. Who created all these? He who brings out the starry hosts one by one and calls them each by name. Because of his great power and mighty strength, not one of them is missing." The same creator who names the stars also knows the names of the seven souls we mourn today.

And the same creator who names the stars knows *your* name as well.

Emily

Sabbath rest

*And by the seventh day God completed His work
which he had done; and he rested on the seventh day
from all His work which He had done.*
Genesis 2:2 NASB

Have you been going hard lately? Maybe it's the daily commute, the Monday through Friday work week, the weekend full of errands and catching up on every other part of your life, or being a mom and having zero days off and zero vacation days. You know what going hard means, don't you? But what about those rare occasions when God gives you an hour, a day or even a weekend free? Do you rest?

God built us to go hard. But He also built us to need rest. That's why He set aside the seventh day as the Sabbath day, a day of rest.

If you've been going hard lately without taking time to rest, talk to God about it. Tell Him that you're tired. Share as much detail about why you're tired as you want to—He's a great listener. Then tell Him that you know He's given you opportunities for a Sabbath rest, but you've been too busy to notice. Say you're sorry. Now ask God to show you divine appointments, opportunities and snatches of time for some Sabbath rest. And when He does show you, seize it. Take a Sabbath. Rest.

Laurie

Strong and mighty

Who is the King of glory? The Lord strong and mighty,
The Lord mighty in battle.
Psalm 24:8 NASB

Some of the strongest people you know may be physically frail. Perhaps they're in wheelchairs, bedridden or taking chemo. Yet the supernatural power and strength of the Holy Spirit overwhelms and overshadows their physical weakness.

Whether you're 18 or 88, whether your health is good or not-so-good, whether you're a single woman, a married woman, a mom, or a grandmother, God's Word says that He is strong and mighty, and through the indwelling power of the Holy Spirit, you also can become stronger and stronger every day of your life.

In the ongoing war between the flesh and the spirit, God has given us strength to face each battle and win. Give Him glory as you prayerfully praise Him for His strength, His power, and His might. There's no age limitation, there's no physical you must pass, and there's no circumstance in life that can disqualify you from experiencing the supernatural, never-ending, all-sufficient, strong and mighty power of the Holy Spirit!

Laurie

Forward faith

Brothers and sisters, I do not consider myself yet to have taken hold of it. But one thing I do: Forgetting what is behind and straining toward what is ahead, I press on toward the goal to win the prize for which God has called me heavenward in Christ Jesus.
Philippians 3:13-14 NIV

Here is the truth about faith. Faith moves in one direction. It moves forward. It does not retreat or go back.

So if you want to determine whether you are living by faith or not, think about your life and think back to when you first came to know Christ. Now think about where you are right now in your walk with Him. Does your life have a forward trajectory? Are you progressing? Do you see yourself growing deeper in the faith and growing more mature spiritually? If you can see progress, even the smallest bit of progress, you can know that it's evidence of God's working in you through faith.

Laurie

Meaningless

*"Everything is meaningless," says the Teacher, "completely
meaningless!"*
Ecclesiastes 1:2 NLT

Do you get frustrated when your tasks are completed and
checked off your To Do list only to reappear moments later?
Within hours the clothes need to be washed again, the floors
need to be mopped again, the bathrooms need to be cleaned
again, and your family is hungry again. When you focus on the
vicious, seemingly futile cycle of your labor, it's easy to throw in
the towel and scream like Solomon, "Everything is meaningless!
Completely meaningless!"

But the life God has given you is not supposed to be a vicious
cycle of futility and dissatisfaction. It is not to be lived with an
earthbound focus. He has redeemed you and given you a life of
joy, purpose, meaning and satisfaction despite your season or
circumstances. However, you can only experience this joyous,
meaningful, satisfying life if you focus on Him and not your
To Do list.

Laurie

Be clear on your assignment

*"Swear by the Lord, the God of heaven and earth,
that you will not allow my son to marry one of these local
Canaanite women. Go instead to my homeland, to my relatives,
and find a wife there for my son Isaac."*
Genesis 24:3-4 NLT

Abraham's servant did not decide to hunt for a wife for Isaac because he thought biblical matchmaking would be fun. He went because he had a direct order from his master.

Before you fix up two singles, check your motives. Are you doing it because you're bored, because you're uncomfortable with someone older still being single, or because you have spent time with God and have truly put it before Him?

Emily

Holy meddling

"O Lord, God of my master, Abraham," he prayed.
"Please give me success today, and show
unfailing love to my master, Abraham."
Genesis 24:12 NLT

Before Abraham's servant even made his first move to find a wife for Isaac, he prayed that God would guide him and that God would provide. He realized that pairing two people together is a very serious, spiritual matter. Therefore, he did not approach matchmaking flippantly or apathetically. He prayed. He sought God's will. And he continued to do so throughout the process.

The Bible says that, "Before he had finished praying, he saw a young woman named Rebekah coming out with her water jug on her shoulder" (v. 15 NLT). Clearly, God cares about holy meddling, because before the servant had even finished praying, God was already answering his prayer.

Emily

Water for camels

> "This is my request. I will ask one of them, 'Please give me
> a drink from your jug.' If she says, 'Yes, have a drink, and
> I will water your camels, too!'—let her be the one you
> have selected as Isaac's wife. This is how I will know
> that you have shown unfailing love to my master."
> Genesis 24:14 NLT

When Abraham's servant prayed for God to help him find a wife for Isaac, he prayed for a woman with a sweet spirit and a strong work ethic. It may seem random that he prayed for a girl who would water his camels, but he knew that someone who went above and beyond what was asked of her would be a woman worthy of his master's son.

What do you consider when you think of a match for your single friend? Someone who makes a lot of money? Who has a good job? Who is attractive and muscular? Or someone with qualities that will really lay the foundation for a strong and solid marriage?

Emily

Don't push the issue

*So they called Rebekah. "Are you willing to go with this man?"
they asked her. And she replied, "Yes, I will go."*
Genesis 24:58 NLT

After Abraham's servant discovered Rebekah and met with her family, he ultimately left the decision up to her. He didn't demand, push or force the issue other than to request that she follow him to Isaac.

Do not be offended if you think two people would be a perfect match and it doesn't ultimately work out. You can't force the issue. You can't make it happen. The best you can do is follow the Lord's prompting and then get out of the way.

Abraham's servant obviously knew what he was doing because the Bible says that after Rebekah became Isaac's wife, "he loved her deeply" (v. 67 NLT). That's a successful match, I'd say!

Emily

Facing opposition

> There is a wide-open door for a great work here,
> although many oppose me.
> 1 Corinthians 16:9 NLT

There's an ugly little secret about doing God's will. Doing God's will is difficult because it always invites and involves opposition. And none of us want that, do we?

So when we read a hard-to-hear passage like 1 Corinthians 16:9, we subconsciously stick our fingers in our ears and do the la-la-la-I-can't-hear-you routine. But the fact remains that doing God's will has always been difficult, and it has always involved opposition It's what Abel experienced from Cain. It's what David experienced from Saul. It's what Jeremiah and the prophets experienced from their own people. It's what Jesus experienced from the angry mob.

From the first pages of Genesis to the final chapters of Revelation, the overwhelming evidence clearly reveals this: Even when God gives you a wide-open door, and even when God calls you to a great work, you will still experience opposition.

So instead of putting your fingers in your ears or sticking your head in the sand, view opposition for what it really is: proof indeed that you really are in God's will.

Laurie

God is...

*Love is patient, love is kind. It does not envy, it does not boast,
it is not proud. It does not dishonor others, it is not self-seeking,
it is not easily angered, it keeps no record of wrongs. Love does not
delight in evil but rejoices with the truth. It always protects,
always trusts, always hopes, always perseveres. Love never fails.*
I Corinthians 13:4-8 NIV

Many people know 1 Corinthians 13 as the "love chapter" of the Bible because it explains, in detail, what love is and how love behaves. But the Bible also says in 1 John 4:8 that "God is love." So because God is love, it makes sense that the "love chapter" of the Bible can also be used to describe God as well:

God is patient, God is kind. He does not envy, He does not boast, He is not proud. He does not dishonor others, He is not self-seeking, He is not easily angered, He keeps no record of wrongs. God does not delight in evil but rejoices with the truth. He always protects, always trusts, always hopes, always perseveres.

God never fails.

What a beautiful description when you put those two truths together.

Emily

Accept and favor your husband

Let your wife be a fountain of blessing for you.
Rejoice in the wife of your youth. She is a loving deer,
a graceful doe. Let her breasts satisfy you always.
May you always be captivated by her love.
Proverbs 5:18–19 NLT

You've probably witnessed the elegance, beauty, and gracefulness of a doe firsthand, and Solomon had all of these qualities in mind when he used this metaphor. But the word "graceful" also denotes "a sense of acceptance or preference,"[4] which gives us an even deeper understanding of this passage. It reveals that a captivating woman graciously accepts her husband and gives him preference—preeminence—above every other earthly relationship.

This same Hebrew word is used to describe God's grace to us— grace we did not earn, grace we did not deserve, grace that loved and reached out to us in spite of our sin. Therefore, in one single phrase from Proverbs 5:19, Solomon is saying that a captivating woman elegantly, beautifully, and graciously accepts her husband just as God accepts us, and she favors him with her love over every earthly rival.

Practically, this means that God wants us to accept our husbands as they are, and to stop focusing on their faults and trying to change them. It also means that He wants us to put our husbands before our children, our family, our friends, our jobs, and every responsibility and possession we have. The only relationship that supersedes our relationship with our husbands is our relationship with Christ (Matt. 10:37).

Laurie

A steamy command

Let your wife be a fountain of blessing for you.
Rejoice in the wife of your youth. She is a loving deer,
a graceful doe. Let her breasts satisfy you always.
May you always be captivated by her love.
Proverbs 5:18–19 NLT

In addition to encouraging you to accept and favor your husband, this passage also has something to say about your intimate relationship with him. It is a pretty steamy passage. The words are infused with fire and intensity. But in reality, this passage is even more sensual in its original Hebrew language.

For example, the Hebrew word "loving" in verse 19 means the wife is a very desirable and passionate lover. The word "love" at the conclusion of this verse is used repeatedly in Song of Solomon, and it refers to the powerful, intimate love between a man and a woman. This is the kind of love God calls us to give to our husbands, and it's much more than mere affection. It is fiery, hot passion.

Laurie

Captivating

> *Let your wife be a fountain of blessing for you.*
> *Rejoice in the wife of your youth. She is a loving deer,*
> *a graceful doe. Let her breasts satisfy you always.*
> *May you always be captivated by her love.*
> Proverbs 5:18–19 NLT

There's one more word we need to examine in this passage. Solomon says the wife in Proverbs 5:19 captivates her husband. But what does "captivate" mean? Very simply, it means "to intoxicate with love."[5] This wife has an absolutely intoxicating effect upon her husband. The power and passion of her love literally makes him reel. The King James Bible translates this word as "ravished," and the New American Standard Bible translates it as "exhilarated." But my favorite translation is the Amplified Bible which says that the husband is "transported with delight in her love." Wow! Now that's some kind of woman and some kind of lovin'!

Laurie

Reconciliation

*For God was pleased to have all his fullness dwell in him,
and through him to reconcile to himself all things,
whether things on earth or things in heaven,
by making peace through his blood, shed on the cross.*
1 Corinthians 1:19-20 NIV

Paul explains in 1 Corinthians that through Jesus' blood that was shed on the cross, God reconciled to Himself all things. In accounting terms, to reconcile something means you bring it into agreement with something else. You may reconcile bank accounts, inventory records or spreadsheets.

Relationships can also be reconciled. When people are "out of balance" or in disagreement, something must be done to get both parties on the same page. With God, sin is the thing that causes us to be in disagreement with Him. It makes your relationship with Him out of balance. But because Jesus paid for your sins on the cross, your relationship with God can be reconciled.

Emily

Everything He inhabits is holy

*Exalt the Lord our God and worship at his holy mountain,
for the Lord our God is holy.*
Psalm 99:9 NIV

God is holy. But not only is God holy, everything He inhabits is too, and within the Bible, His holiness spills over into an array of ancillary realities that are also described as holy:

- His throne
- His mountain
- His arm
- His temple
- His way
- His city
- His Spirit
- Even His name

Because God is holy, He demands that we be holy too. On the surface, this seems like the most unattainable command in the entire Bible. But when we remember that whatever God inhabits is also holy, the command comes within reach. You cannot be holy on your own strength; it is only attained by embracing His holiness as He inhabits you.

Emily

February 17

Q & A session

*Why are you in despair, O my soul? And why
have you become disturbed within me? Hope in God,
for I shall again praise Him for the help of His presence.*
Psalm 42:5 NASB

Look closely at today's Psalm. Do you see it? The Psalmist is talking to himself—in a very healthy way, of course. Actually he's asking himself a couple of questions—really good questions. Then he gives himself some excellent advice and reminds himself of the hope and help he has in God.

Maybe you need to have a little question and answer session with yourself today. Ask yourself, "Why am I worrying today? Why have I become upset and fearful?" Then activate your faith by believing and praising the Lord for His hope, His help and His presence in your life.

Laurie

Your story

Let the redeemed of the Lord tell their story.
Psalm 107:2 NIV

We all have a story to share. How did you come to know the Lord? What is He doing in your life right now? What are some miracles you've witnessed during your lifetime, and how has He provided for you? Those are your stories.

Perhaps you think your story (or your testimony as some call it) isn't dramatic enough. Or maybe you think yours is too dramatic. Stop worrying. If you have been redeemed, say so! It's not your job to question the outcome of sharing your story; it's just your job to tell it.

Emily

February 19

Love first

Then Jesus stood up again and said to the woman,
"Where are your accusers? Didn't even one of
them condemn you?" "No, Lord," she said.
And Jesus said, "Neither do I. Go and sin no more."
John 8:10-11 NLT

When Jesus encountered people who were caught in sin, like the woman who was caught in adultery, He first showed them love and then He told them to go and sin no more. He didn't insist that they stop sinning first.

It is important for Christians to address sin and expose it for what it is, but we must be careful not to offer a symphony of condemnation without an overture of love. Love must come first. When a person accepts the love of God and turns her life to Him, actions begin to change on their own. So address sin, yes. But open with love like Jesus.

Emily

Tune your ears to wisdom

Tune your ears to wisdom, and concentrate on understandings.
Proverbs 2:2 NLT

If you've ever used Pandora Radio, you know that it provides a way to completely personalize your music experience. You can create your own stations based on the songs, artists and albums you like, and Pandora will recommend new songs and artists that are "genetically similar" to your favorites. The more feedback you give, the more specialized your station will become.

Unfortunately, the world is not like Pandora Radio. It doesn't allow you to get more of what you like and filter everything else out. Instead, it throws all sorts of advice and information in your direction and it's up to you to determine if it's "genetically similar" to the truth that God provides in His Word.

Thankfully, you have the Holy Spirit who is a filter for truth just like Pandora is a filter for music. The more you listen to God's wisdom, the more your ears will be able to recognize wisdom when you hear it.

Laurie

Love with actions

*Dear children, let us not love with words or tongue
but with actions and in truth.*
1 John 3:18 NIV

God gives us experiences and trials for a reason. One of those reasons is to instill empathy into our lives that we may reach and help others who are going through similar trials. That we may show His love with our actions.

What about you? Do you seek out opportunities to minister to others based on the trials you've experienced yourself? Do you see a need and act upon it immediately? Do you go the extra mile? Sometimes it means simply sharing your umbrella. And other times it means running out in the rain, getting drenched and showing the world what God's love really looks like.

Emily

Seek Him first

But seek first his kingdom and his righteousness,
and all these things will be given to you as well.
Matthew 6:33 NIV

You don't have to settle for a less-than-best life. But in order to experience the best God has in store for you, you must stop setting your heart on seeking secondary stuff first. Even good priorities, like your marriage, your family, your career or your passion for ministry must be pushed aside so God Himself can have ultimate priority.

God does not want second place in your life. He wants first place. But when you put Him first, amazing things will happen. Your life may not become perfect or problem-free, but He will give you the life you've always wanted—a life full of joy and peace.

Laurie

To sojourn

*Now it came about in the days when the judges governed,
that there was a famine in the land. And a certain man
of Bethlehem in Judah went to sojourn in the land of Moab
with his wife and his two sons. The name of the man was
Elimelech, and the name of his wife, Naomi; and the names of
his two sons were Mahlon and Chilion, Ephrathites of Bethlehem
in Judah. Now they entered the land of Moab and remained there.*
Ruth 1:1-2 NIV

The story of Ruth begins with one man's decision to travel outside of the will of God. For years the Israelites were wanderers, but once they finally entered into the Promise Land, they were supposed to stay there. Being in the Promise Land was synonymous with being in the direct will of God. So when Elimelech decided to move his family from Bethlehem to Moab, not only did he bring them out of the Promise Land, he also brought them out of God's will.

What's most interesting, though, is that Elimelech's intentions were to "sojourn" in Moab, or to stay there only temporarily. Instead, the Bible says they "remained there." Most people never intend to remain outside the will of God. However, a temporary visit leads to a permanent residence.

Emily

Christ in you

Christ in you, the hope of glory.
Colossians 1:27 NASB

You may imagine that when the Israelites witnessed God's visible presence in the form of a cloud by day and a pillar of fire by night, the awesome glory of God's presence must have dazzled them day and night. But the truth is, they probably took God's presence for granted, just like we do.

They probably got up and went outside some mornings to gather "the usual," manna. Then they made breakfast and began going about their ordinary daily routine. That evening they had their quail dinner, cleaned the dishes and put the kids to bed. Then they tucked themselves in and nodded off to sleep, never even conscious of the fiery pillar of God's presence illuminating the night skies above them. I imagine that from time to time a woman might even whisper to her husband right before they fell asleep, "Honey, you know, I didn't notice, but was the cloud out today?"

Christ, the hope of glory, is in you! You embody the very presence of God. But has that become so ordinary that you take it for granted? Pray that He will reawaken you to the wonder of His presence in you. Because His presence in you is far better than any cloud or fiery pillar!

Laurie

God knows the heart

And he who searches our hearts knows the mind of the Spirit,
because the Spirit intercedes for God's people
in accordance with the will of God.
Romans 8:27 NIV

Have you ever wished you could change someone?

Maybe you have a family member who is ruining his life with alcohol or drugs. Maybe you can't have a conversation with your mother without facing a guilt trip or criticism. Maybe your boss is just impossible to handle.

It's frustrating to watch someone you love ruin his or her life. You want to help. You want to reason with them. You want them to see that God has a better way. But no matter how eloquent or sincere you are, they refuse to see the light.

It's important to remember that you cannot change another person's heart. You can address their behavior, but only God knows their hearts and only He can initiate change from the inside out.

Thank the Lord that the person you see as impossible to change is not your responsibility anyway.

Emily

Face to face

*The Lord would speak to Moses face to face,
as one speaks to a friend.*
Exodus 33:11 NIV

One of the reasons Moses was so intimate with God was that he was so dependent upon God's presence and power. Faced with the constant, overwhelming challenges of leading God's people, Moses responded with a constant, overwhelming hunger to know and experience God.

Are you completely dependent upon God's presence and power in your daily life? Do you have an overwhelming hunger to know and experience God in an intimate way? Today, express the desire of your heart to God.

Laurie

February 27

Consider encouragement

*And let us consider how we may spur
one another on toward love and good deeds.*
Hebrews 10:24 NIV

Everyone needs a spiritual cheerleader. Everyone longs for a pep rally before they face the day. Even the most independent, self-sufficient person has a fundamental need for encouragement.

But encouragement does not happen accidentally. It takes planning, forethought, thinking and follow through. If you want to be an encourager, you must be intentional. Consider those closest to you and think about how they need to be encouraged. What can you say or do to encourage them today?

Emily

The divisive

And now I make one more appeal, my dear brothers and sisters.
Watch out for people who cause divisions and upset people's
faith by teaching things contrary to what you have been taught.
Stay away from them.
Romans 16:17 NLT

When you read about fellow believers who are divisive, someone specific probably comes to your mind. Someone who enjoys heated discussions. Someone who thrives on stirring up dissension. If you're a peacemaker by nature, you may be tempted to put up with such people and may even feel that it's easiest just to ignore them altogether. But Paul warns us not to ignore them at all. We should keep our distance, but we should also keep our eyes on them as well. These people are dangerous because they have the potential to upset people's faith. So we must be on guard. We must be cautious. We must not turn a blind eye to them in the spirit of maintaining the peace.

Laurie

march

Protect your peaches

*Be of sober spirit, be on the alert. Your adversary, the devil,
prowls around like a roaring lion, seeking someone to devour.
But resist him, firm in your faith.*
1 Peter 5:8-9 NASB

When you have a peach tree, you have to fight many worthy adversaries who want those ripe, juicy peaches just as much as you do: birds, deer, raccoons. Critters from all over will keep their eyes on your tree so they can destroy its fruit before you get to it. Those who are serious about their peaches will go out of their way to protect them with makeshift weapons like wind chimes to scare away the animals.

You may not have a peach tree, but you do have fruit you need to protect, the fruit of the Spirit. "But the fruit of the Spirit is love, joy, peace, patience, kindness, goodness, faithfulness, gentleness, self-control" (Gal. 5:22-23 NASB). Your adversary, the devil, is out to destroy your fruit just like the animals want to destroy your peaches. But it will take more than wind chimes to scare him away. It will take the armor of God (Ephesians 6). Be alert. Put on the armor of God, and protect your fruit.

Laurie

Conform your will

Do not conform to the pattern of this world, but be transformed by the renewing of your mind. Then you will be able to test and approve what God's will is—his good, pleasing and perfect will.
Romans 12:2 NIV

Sometimes God's will does not seem good, pleasing *or* perfect. When Jesus prayed for God's will to be done in the Garden of Gethsemane, He demonstrated just how difficult submitting to God's will can be. So difficult, in fact, that sometimes you have to pray over and over again, just as He did.

The first time you pray, "Not my will, but Yours," you may not even mean it at all. You may have to say it with clenched fists through gritted teeth. But the divine nature of this prayer is that each time you whisper it, your own will slowly looses power until eventually, you really mean what you're praying. Your mind is renewed, your heart is transformed, and your own will is conformed to His.

Emily

Before you lead

Lord, our Lord, how majestic is your name in all the earth!
You have set your glory in the heavens.
Psalm 8:1 NIV

You are a leader. John Maxwell, author and expert on leadership, says, "Leadership is influence," and because your life influences others—your family, friends, co-workers, etc.—you're a leader.

But before you can lead well, you must follow well. Consider King David. Long before he ever led others, he led sheep—not a prestigious job. But during those days before becoming a powerful, well-known king, David followed God and cultivated a close relationship with Him. You can see the evidence of this intimacy in Psalm 8, a psalm he wrote when he was just a young shepherd.

If you want your influence over others to lead them closer to the Lord, start by giving your relationship with God priority.

Laurie

Marching

*You shall march around the city, all the men of war
circling the city once. You shall do so for six days.*
Joshua 6:3 NASB

Before Joshua and his army conquered Jericho, they had to march around the city for six days. I imagine there were at least a few who questioned such a tactic. Shouldn't they be doing more? Couldn't they charge the city *now*?

Not every moment with the Lord is going to be a climactic event in which walls come tumbling down. Sometimes it's just going to be marching. Boring, ho-hum, one foot in front of the other marching. But no matter how pointless it seems, there is value in the marching. We do the "small" things—like march around a city, attend church, or read our Bibles—so that when He calls on us to blow our trumpets in battle, we are ready! We don't have to dig in the bottom of our closets for the trumpets and then dust them off. We're ready and we're prepared because we have marched faithfully.

Emily

Press play

And now, dear brothers and sisters, one final thing.
Fix your thoughts on what is true, and honorable, and right,
and pure, and lovely, and admirable. Think about things
that are excellent and worthy of praise.
Philippians 4:8 NLT

Just like you have favorite radio stations preset in your car, you also have your favorite thoughts preset in your mind. If your inmost thoughts are true, honorable, right, and pure, your life will reveal it. But if the channels you listen to are bitter, corrupt, slanderous, and impure, your life will reflect that as well.

One of the truest ways you can know whether you're progressing or regressing spiritually is by the thoughts you purposefully "play." What do your current thoughts reveal about your own spiritual condition? Is it time for you to reprogram the preset buttons in your mind?

Laurie

It could happen

*We all, like sheep, have gone astray, each of us has turned
to our own way; and the Lord has laid on him the iniquity of us all.*
Isaiah 53:6 NIV

Many life-destroying sins could be avoided if you just do two simple things. The first is to admit that it could happen to you. The Bible says that we're all like sheep, prone to wander away from our shepherd. Your spirit may be willing to obey, but your flesh is oh-so-weak. Satan wants you to think it could never happen to you, but greater men (and women) have fallen.

Second, you must avoid the first step. Satan doesn't bother tempting you to take big jumps into sin. "Here! Try heroin! Have an affair! Embezzle from your boss! Marry a non-believer!" Instead, he hooks you with those seemingly insignificant first steps and then patiently waits until you take the next, and the next, and the next. "It's just a cigarette. He's only a Facebook friend. It's just a few office supplies. It's only one date. It's just a silly book. It's just a silly movie."

Once you admit that you're not above those life-destroying sins, and once you choose to avoid those "harmless" first steps, many gray-area decisions will become quite easy for you to make.

Emily

Temporary structure

The Most High doesn't live in temples made by human hands.
Acts 7:48 NLT

It is significant that the Old Testament tabernacle was a temporal structure. It was never intended to be a permanent structure, and eventually it was replaced by Solomon's temple (which was also temporary).

This temporal aspect of the tabernacle showed the Israelites that "the Most High doesn't live in temples made by human hands," and it foreshadowed a time when God's presence would inhabit temporal, human "tents" as well.

The only permanent "structure" that the Lord inhabits is the hearts of His people. He doesn't inhabit your church; He inhabits the people who attend your church. He doesn't inhabit your house; He inhabits the people who live in your house.

Laurie

Let's get physical

And all the people were trying to touch Him…
Luke 6:19 NASB

You know that God is everywhere, but don't you wish you could feel Him sometimes? Don't you wish you could experience His presence physically instead of just spiritually? It's not like you can touch Him. You can't hug Him. He's not going to give you a love pat on your rump after your quiet time huddle and then send you on your way to face the next play in life. How can God be everywhere at once, yet you're still not able to touch Him?

The desire to touch God is the very reason why we need other believers in our lives. We sometimes forget that they can be "God with skin on" to us. God may not come down and physically hug you, but He can send a friend along your path to hug you just when you need it most. He may not kiss you, but when your child sees you crying, He may lead him to kiss your cheek. Each hug, each kiss, each pat on the back can be a touch from God through the arms of one of His children.

If you're feeling alone, begin praying that He will allow you to experience His presence in a physical way. If you need a hug, pray for a hug. If you need help with the dishes, pray for it. If you need to experience God with skin on, pray for His presence to appear in tangible ways that you can recognize and appreciate.

Emily

Discern what is best

And this is my prayer: that your love may abound more and more in knowledge and depth of insight, so that you may be able to discern what is best and may be pure and blameless for the day of Christ.
Philippians 1:9-10 NIV

Having a favorite pair of blue jeans is like having gold! Once you find the perfect pair, it becomes your default clothing when you're not quite sure what else to wear.

Some Bible verses have the same effect. There are many times when you face an issue that does not have a clear right or wrong answer in Scripture. Issues like, *How many children should we have?* or *Should I volunteer for this ministry?* In those cases, Paul provides this wonderful "blue jean verse" that you can default to anytime you're not quite sure what else to pray.

Instead of wrestling with the Lord through those uncertainties that don't always end in right or wrong, pray like Paul did and ask Him to help you discern what is *best*.

Emily

Old, gray and beautiful

Now that I am old and gray, do not abandon me, O God.
Let me proclaim your power to this new generation,
your mighty miracles to all who come after me.
Psalm 71:18 NLT

Most women do not plan to become bitter, selfish, negative old ladies when they age, but we've all met those who are. Thankfully, there's no better day than today to begin becoming the old woman you want to be. Here's how:

• By proclaiming God's "power to this new generation" today and every remaining day of your life (Ps. 71:18).

• By living a godly lifestyle and walking with Him today and every day so that in your old age you will still produce fruit (Ps. 92:14).

• By singing and praising the Lord today, tomorrow and every day thereafter so that the final whispers from your wrinkled lips will be the sweet sounds of His praise (Ps. 104:33).

Laurie

Inner circle

They went to a place called Gethsemane,
and Jesus said to his disciples, "Sit here while I pray."
He took Peter, James and John along with him, and
he began to be deeply distressed and troubled. "My soul
is overwhelmed with sorrow to the point of death,"
he said to them. "Stay here and keep watch."
Mark 14:32-34 NIV

In Jesus' inner circle of friendship, we see three people: Peter, James and John. Of everyone Jesus associated with, these were the three who were closest to Him. Jesus shared things with Peter, James and John that He didn't share with anyone else. He confided in them. He trusted them. He formed unbreakable bonds with them.

But notice how small Jesus' inner circle was. Just three friends.

You may yearn for more friendships and be frustrated that there are only one or two people you can go to who truly understand you. But if you have just a couple of friends—over the course of your entire lifetime—who fit into this category, you should still consider yourself blessed. These "inner circle" friends are 100% quality and 0% quantity. Do not be so eager to invite people into this circle. It is sacred, and it is holy. And these relationships, when they do come, are to be cherished and protected.

Emily

God loves change

> *Listen, I tell you a mystery: We will not all sleep,*
> *but we will all be changed—in a flash, in the twinkling*
> *of an eye, at the last trumpet. For the trumpet will sound,*
> *the dead will be raised imperishable, and we will be changed.*
> 1 Corinthians 15:51-52 NIV

God loves change.

He uses change to change us, and change glorifies Him. He loves change because change is a chisel He can use to change us, and because changed lives glorify Him.

Without change, our hearts would very likely become calloused and cool, prideful and self-sufficient. Without change, we'd probably be spiritually stunted, carnal, and immature. But change brings us to our knees, drives us to His Word, and compels us to depend desperately upon our Father. When we choose to respond to change like that, our hearts become tender, our love for God grows, and our lives are transformed—changed—giving evidence of God's power and glory.

Yes, God loves change.

Laurie

One more time

How sweet your words taste to me;
they are sweeter than honey.
Psalm 119:103 NLT

I used to think that reading the whole Bible was a one-time right-of-passage for Christians. It was kind of like: 1) Get saved (check). 2) Get baptized (check). 3) Read the Bible (check).

Perhaps you've already read the Bible once, but you're having a hard time motivating yourself to read it again. The first time you were fueled by determination and passion and the excitement of discovering something new. But the second time, it may be a little harder to manufacture that focus that you had before.

If you truly want to get the Word of God rooted in you, this is where the roots start to go deep—by *repeated reading of the Word of God.* By becoming familiar with it. By knowing it. By reading it over and over and over again.

No matter how many times you've read the Bible before, read it *one more time.* If you've never read it or if you've read it twenty times, read it one more time.

Emily

Movable, portable

> *I have never lived in a house, from the day I brought*
> *the Israelites out of Egypt until this very day.*
> *I have always moved from one place to another*
> *with a tent and a Tabernacle as my dwelling.*
> 2 Samuel 7:6 NLT

The tabernacle was designed by God to be a portable, movable structure. All throughout the Israelites' journey to Canaan, the tabernacle moved with them from place to place. This aspect of the tabernacle taught them about their need for God's continual presence and about the reality of God's omnipresence. It also foreshadowed our need for God to dwell within us and to journey with us through our daily pilgrimage here on earth.

God moves with you from place to place, from moment to moment. He does not plant His feet and wait for you to find Him. He is omnipresent, dwelling within you, able to journey with you no matter where you go.

Laurie

Meeting needs from the cross

*When Jesus saw his mother there, and the disciple whom he loved
standing nearby, he said to her, "Woman, here is your son,"
and to the disciple, "Here is your mother." From that time on,
this disciple took her into his home.*
John 19:26-27 NIV

There is one thing that happened in the shadow of the
cross that often gets overlooked. Jesus spoke specifically
to His disciple, John, and to His mother, Mary. He said to Mary,
"Here is your son," and to John, "Here is your mother."

He did this because, as the oldest son, Jesus had an obligation
to care for His mother in the absence of His father, Joseph.
By transferring that responsibility to His disciple, John, Jesus made
sure that His mother would be cared for after His death.

Even from the cross, Jesus' heart and thoughts were on taking
care of others and providing for their needs. When you live
in the shadow of the cross, you also can have peace that God will
supply all of your needs.

Emily

*In my Father's house are many mansions: if it were not so,
I would have told you. I go to prepare a place for you.*
John 14:2 KJV

Heaven. It's a land beyond our comprehension. It's a city custom-designed by the greatest architect of all time. It's built by the One who laid the foundation of the world. It's created by the master carpenter whose nail-pierced hands bear the scars of our sins. His budget is unlimited. His materials are priceless. And He bought and paid for it all with His blood. It's heaven. It's home. And it's glorious because, best of all…He'll be there!

Laurie

What's your pig?

*A woman who is beautiful but lacks discretion
is like a gold ring in a pig's snout.*
Proverbs 11:22 NLT

Do you frequently call your husband at work and whine about the difficult day you're having? Do you meet him at the door with a list of catastrophes that occurred during the day? There are a number of elements that play in to becoming a woman of discretion, but one that often gets overlooked is the issue of timing. Becoming a woman of discretion is not just about paying attention to *what* you say and *how* you say it; it's also about paying attention to *when* you say it.

You may have mastered gossip, put-downs, sarcasm and yelling. Your tone of voice may be as sweet as honey. But could it be that you still have one "pig" left to conquer? Even the right thing said at the wrong time can be like a gold ring in a pig's snout.

Emily

Submit to authority

"You are more righteous than I," [Saul] said.
"You have treated me well, but I have treated you badly."
I Samuel 24:17 NIV

Even leaders have to submit to authority. As a young man, David was submissive to his father, Jesse, and throughout his years of service to King Saul, David was submissive to him as well. Even when Saul's jealousy drove him to destroy David, David continued to treat Saul with respect.

If you want to be an effective leader, you must set the example by respecting and submitting to those who are in authority over you. They may not deserve it. They may even take advantage of it. But it is still your responsibility to submit to them because their poor leadership does not excuse you from their authority.

Laurie

Truth as a girdle

Stand firm therefore, having girded your loins with truth…
Ephesians 6:14 NASB

To "gird" something means to surround or encircle it, and this is where we get the word for the ever-so-unpopular woman's accessory—the girdle. So when we put the belt of truth alongside what we know to be true about girdles, Paul's command takes on a slightly different, more challenging meaning.

To simply wrap yourself in truth may not necessarily be enough. It somehow implies that truth, even though it may go all the way around your middle, still lies somewhat awkwardly and loosely, held together only by a cheap buckle or a sloppy bow. But if you *gird* yourself in truth, truth becomes like a second skin, hugging you so tightly and snugly that those who look at you don't see you at all. Instead they see truth. The outline of truth. The form of truth. The shape of truth.

Emily

Avoid the devoid

Work willingly at whatever you do, as though you were working for the Lord rather than for people.
Colossians 3:23 NLT

In every season, you're going to face meaningless tasks and daily frustrations that seem futile and completely devoid of purpose. It may be sitting in traffic, updating spreadsheets, mowing the grass or cleaning potties. But as difficult as these pointless things may feel, you must be careful about the way you deal with them because they can easily and quickly suck the joy out of your life. They can make you want to respond in ways that would be hurtful to others and hurtful to the kingdom of God.

Instead, you must trust the words of Colossians 3:23 and do whatever grunt work you must with your whole, undivided heart. You must do it unto the Lord—not for yourself and certainly not for others—in order to have any hope of maintaining joy. When you do, it is transforming. Traffic becomes an altar and potties become thrones.

Laurie

Controllers

But Peter took him aside and began to reprimand him for saying such things. "Heaven forbid, Lord," he said. "This will never happen to you!" Jesus turned to Peter and said, "Get away from me, Satan! You are a dangerous trap to me. You are seeing things merely from a human point of view, not from God's."
Matthew 16:22-23 NLT

There may be some people in your life who have an opinion about everything you should or should not do. Their intentions may be good and they may love you very much, just like Peter loved Jesus, but they still want to be the ones controlling your life.

If you're following the Lord and these people start telling you that you should be doing something differently, you need to stand your ground. You must follow Jesus' example and resist these strong personalities. Speak the truth to them in love, but be firm in your decision to remain in God's will. Even the most well-intentioned people can cause you to stray from God's plans and to compromise your obedience to Him. Do not crumble under the pressure. Stand your ground and do not be controlled by anyone but God.

Laurie

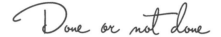
Done or not done

> *"Ah Lord God! Behold, You have made the heavens and the earth*
> *by Your great power and by Your outstretched arm!*
> *Nothing is too difficult for You."*
> Jeremiah 32:17 NASB

Sometimes we think that miracles—the things that God does which are outside of the natural laws of the universe—are the best examples of God's power. They are the things we like to talk about. They are the things we pray for. They are the times when we feel God really shows up!

- Creation. *Awesome display of power.*
- The virgin birth. *Greatest miracle ever.*
- Destruction of Jericho. *Awesome!*
- Calming the storm. *So cool!*

But when it comes to God's power, miracles do not show a greater degree of God's power. They just show God's constant, unchanging, consistent power in a different way. Miracles are not difficult for God any more than making grass grow is easy for Him. With God, there is no easy or difficult, no natural or miraculous.

There is only done or not done.

Emily

March 23

Start with obedience

Then Jesus came from Galilee to the Jordan to be baptized by John.
Matthew 3:13 NIV

I think it's interesting that Jesus' public ministry did not begin with a big speech or a publicity campaign announcing, "Here He is. Your long-awaited Messiah has finally come!" In fact, Jesus did not even begin His ministry by preaching an impressive sermon at the local synagogue. Instead, Jesus chose to begin His ministry in a very symbolic, deeply significant way, and, oh, how God was glorified!

Jesus started His ministry with obedience. Obedience to be baptized. Obedience to set an example. Obedience to begin at the beginning and rely on God for every step.

Obedience is not a step you can skip. Whether your ministry is a global one reaching thousands of people for the gospel or a simple one reaching just one small child, you must first and foremost start your ministry with obedience.

Laurie

Spring cleaning

In his pride the wicked man does not seek him;
in all his thoughts there is no room for God.
Psalm 10:4 NIV

Your mind is probably as full as a closet in desperate need of spring cleaning with a million thoughts all begging to be organized. But in all of those thoughts, is there room for God? Where does your mind wander during those long, weekly meetings at the office? As the warm water from your morning shower massages your neck and your back? In the silence as you lie on your back and stare into the darkness before finally closing your eyes at night? Do you relive the day's events and analyze each moment, or do you thank God for giving you those moments? Do you worry if tomorrow's plans will go smoothly, or do you contemplate the God who has already orchestrated eternity?

Don't let it be said of you that in all your thoughts, there was no room for God. Clean out the closet of your mind. Throw away all those worries and think on God. Throw out regret and think on God. Rid yourself of life's distractions and instead think on God. For, just as scrubbing and polishing helps our home reflect the summer sun, so will a little spring cleaning of our mind help us to reflect the Son.

Emily

Help, don't hinder

And I ask you, my true partner, to help these two women,
for they worked hard with me in telling others the Good News.
Philippians 4:3 NLT

When two people have a disagreement and you're caught in the middle, you basically have two choices. You can help them, or you can hinder them.

It may be tempting to take sides. You may want to throw your opinion into the mix. But Paul says stop. Don't add fuel to the fire by getting caught up in all of the pettiness that can come from a minor disagreement. Don't say or do anything that will prohibit communication or prolong their reconciliation. Instead, when you're on the outside looking in, "help these two women" find common ground so that they can work together once again to proclaim the good news.

Laurie

Spotting a counterfeit

All a person's ways seem pure to them,
but motives are weighed by the Lord.
Proverbs 16:2 NIV

When people try to counterfeit currency, there are many ways they may try to add the red and blue security features to their counterfeit bills. The difference between many fake and real bills, however, is that authentic paper money has the red and blue security fibers embedded into the very fibers of the fabric pulp before it even becomes paper. The security fibers are not added to the bills; they are a part of the bills.

Likewise, it is not enough for us to do the right thing on the surface. When Jesus sanctifies us, He doesn't seek to influence our actions. He digs deeper and deeper to influence our very motives. It's not enough to sprinkle sanctification on the surface of our lives. It must be embedded into our very being.

Emily

Who to forgive

Be kind and compassionate to one another,
forgiving each other, just as in Christ God forgave you.
Ephesians 4:32 NIV

The Bible tells of two instances of forgiveness that occurred while Jesus was being crucified on the cross. The first is when Jesus forgave those who were executing Him. "Father, forgive them, for they do not know what they are doing" (Luke 23:32-34). The second is when Jesus forgave the criminal who was being crucified beside Him. "Jesus answered him, 'Truly I tell you, today you will be with me in paradise'" (Luke 23:39-43).

One person repented and asked for forgiveness. The others showed no signs of repentance and kept doing wrong. Jesus forgave both.

To forgive as Christ forgave is to forgive everyone who has wronged you, regardless of whether or not they repent or say they're sorry.

Emily

Dare to hope

Yet I still dare to hope when I remember this:
The faithful love of the Lord never ends! His mercies never cease.
Lamentations 3:21-22 NLT

The beauty of walking with Christ is that we can dare to hope even in the darkest circumstances. We can dare to hope because His compassion never ends. His lovingkindness never ceases. His mercy never fails.

When you're sick and everyone else is ready for you to get well, when you're going through a hard time and everyone else is ready for you to get over it, or when you're sad and everyone else is ready for you to slap a smile on your face and get on with life, God's love and patience only increases. If you're still carrying around a heartbreak or a heaviness in your soul, you can dare to hope in a God whose love, mercy and compassion have no limits.

Laurie

No whine

> *Do everything without complaining or arguing.*
> Philippians 2:14 NIV

If ever a group of people knew how to whine and complain, it was the Israelites. After God had done so much for them, I am amazed at how quickly they began to complain. In the passages surrounding Exodus 16, there is a reference to the Israelites' grumbling almost ten times! Keep in mind, this group of people had just witnessed one of the greatest miracles ever—the parting of the Red Sea. They had survived the ten plagues against the Egyptians and then marched across dry land to escape captivity; and the second they were free, they began to complain. They complained about the water, about the manna, about their leaders. They even whined because they weren't in captivity anymore.

And, as silly and ungrateful as the Israelites look to us today, frequently we're no better than they were. God answers our prayers day after day as He fulfills His promise to take care of us. Yet the minute something doesn't go exactly according to our plan, we grumble and complain. Perhaps we should all take a "non-alcoholic" approach to life from now on by cutting the "whine" from our lips. "Do everything without complaining or arguing, so that you may become blameless and pure, children of God without fault in a crooked and depraved generation, in which you shine like stars in the universe" (Phil. 2:14-15 NIV).

Emily

Catch all the foxes, those little foxes, before they ruin the
vineyard of love, for the grapevines are blossoming!
Song of Solomon 2:15 NLT

Many times, there are things in your marriage that appear to be insignificant on the surface, but when multiplied, they have the potential to destroy your marriage. Things like sarcasm, disrespect, or indifference. King Solomon refers to things like these as "little foxes" that "ruin the vineyard of love."

What are some "little foxes" that can ruin and prevent love from blossoming in your marriage? What are you doing to catch them before they ruin your vineyard?

Laurie

Prayer for pastors

*I urge you, brothers and sisters, by our Lord Jesus Christ
and by the love of the Spirit, to join me in my struggle
by praying to God for me.*
Romans 15:30 NIV

While Paul wasn't a pastor like our modern-day pastors with an office and a staff and a closet full of ties, he still led a body of believers. And as he wrote to those believers in his letters we refer to as Ephesians, Philippians, etc., he continually asked for one thing: Prayer.

- *Pray also for me, that whenever I speak, words may be given me so that I will fearlessly make known the mystery of the gospel* (Eph. 6:19 NIV).

- *And pray for us, too, that God may open a door for our message, so that we may proclaim the mystery of Christ, for which I am in chains* (Col. 4:3 NIV).

- *As for other matters, brothers and sisters, pray for us that the message of the Lord may spread rapidly and be honored, just as it was with you* (2 Thess. 3:1 NIV).

Paul was very transparent in his need for prayers from fellow believers. He needed them. He longed for them. He drew strength from them. And his requests for prayer remind us that our Christian leaders need them today as well. Whether they are mega-pastors, Christian musicians or your local small-town worship leader, they want and need your prayers.

Emily

April

Spiritual high

*So the people of Israel walked through the middle of the sea
on dry ground, with walls of water on each side!*
Exodus 14:22 NLT

There is a "low" that often follows a spiritual "high." It can come after mission trips, church camp, retreats, conferences and revivals. Think of it as the wilderness that comes after the Red Sea.

On the list of the top ten spiritual highs, I'm sure that seeing a whole body of water separate like a zipper just long enough for you and thousands of your closest family members to walk across it would be among the top three. However, it was followed by another forty years of wandering before the Israelites claimed the Promise Land. Why?

They allowed their spiritual high to melt into a morning-after feeling of regret, doubt and confusion about the future.

If you're not careful, your own spiritual high can morph into a season of wandering just like the Israelites. Thankfully, it is possible to maintain your spiritual high and avoid a season of wandering by remembering that God's faithfulness never melts away.

Emily

Wisdom and joy

*And so, my children, listen to me (wisdom),
for all who follow my ways are joyful…
Joyful are those who listen to me, watching for me
daily at my gates, waiting for me outside my home!*
Proverbs 8:32, 34 NLT

Everyone wants to have joy, and those who follow wisdom usually do. Take a few minutes to praise and thank God for the joy He has brought you, and for the sorrow He has saved you from all because of the wisdom He has given you.

Laurie

Praise without understanding

The centurion, seeing what had happened, praised God and said,
"Surely this was a righteous man."
Luke 23:47 NIV

Matthew 27:54 tells of a Roman guard who stood in the shadow of the cross on the day of Jesus' crucifixion. After Jesus died, he exclaimed, "Surely he was the Son of God!" Luke goes on to say that the centurion watched what happened and "praised God." This is significant because, aside from acknowledging Jesus as the son of God, the Roman guard probably didn't understand much else about Jesus. He was not a Jew and did not have the same understanding of the Messiah as many of the Jews did. However, what he witnessed led him to praise God despite his limited understanding.

Are you able to praise God even when you don't fully understand Him? Or is your praise dependent upon logic and reason? You may have questions about what God is doing in your life. His ways may not make sense and you may not understand His motivations. But do not let that stop you from praising Him anyway. Stand in the shadow of the cross like the centurion did and praise God despite your limited understanding.

Emily

Be His disciple

Then Jesus said to his disciples, "Whoever wants to be my disciple must deny themselves and take up their cross and follow me."
Matthew 16:24 NIV

Jesus calls us to be disciples. But although all disciples are Christians, all Christians are not disciples.

1 John 2:28 says that you should "remain in fellowship with Christ so that when he returns, you will be full of courage and not shrink back from him in shame" (NLT). Are you remaining in fellowship with Him? What if He surprised you and came back today? Would He find you thriving—*glo*-ing and growing—in your walk with Him? If you are His disciple, then yes, He would.

Precious sister, do not hesitate. And do not settle for a watered-down, lukewarm version of Christianity either. Accept the invitation of a lifetime. Follow Jesus. Be His disciple.

Laurie

Outer circle

While Jesus was having dinner at Matthew's house, many tax collectors and sinners came and ate with him and his disciples. When the Pharisees saw this, they asked his disciples, "Why does your teacher eat with tax collectors and sinners?" On hearing this, Jesus said, "It is not the healthy who need a doctor, but the sick."
Matthew 9:10-12 NIV

The Bible is very clear—Jesus was friendly toward everyone, the sinner and the saint. He did not cut people out of His life who did not believe in Him; instead, He showed them love, ministered to them, and even went so far as to share meals with them. To the Pharisees, this was scandalous.

But Jesus' example can teach us something about friendship. While He remained friendly and loving toward everyone, He still maintained a healthy relational distance between Himself and those in His outer circle.

While it's biblical to be friendly toward everyone, you should still follow Jesus' example and maintain a healthy distance between yourself and the people in your outer circle who do not share your spiritual beliefs. What is a healthy distance? It is the distance to which you have influence on them, but they do not have influence on you.

Emily

Evidence of God

*In the past [God] permitted all the nations to go their own ways,
but he never left them without evidence of himself and his goodness.
For instance, he sends you rain and good crops and gives you
food and joyful hearts.*
Acts 14:16-17 NLT

Every nation and generation has witnessed the evidence of God and His goodness. According to Acts 14:17, His goodness is in the rain that pours down from heaven. It's in the crops and the food that we eat. Even the joy that we feel in our hearts testifies to the evidence of God.

Today may not hold a lot of promise for you. You may feel that God is far away and uninvolved or unconcerned about the details of your life. But Acts 14:17 can be the door that transforms your black-and-white day into a full-color encounter with the evidence of God. Open your door. Step outside. The evidence of God is all around you and it's easier to see than you think.

Laurie

Every single word

*My eyes stay open through the watches of the night,
that I may meditate on your promises.*
Psalm 119:148 NIV

There are times when I read my Bible quickly and lazily, flying over the words like a crop duster. I skim the surface just enough to get the main idea, but don't settle on anything long enough to feel the weight of each individual word. Not surprisingly, I don't get much out of those times of reading. But other times, when I slow down and prayerfully consider every word and detail as I'm reading, God's Word seems to jump off the page and settle into my heart.

What about you? How carefully are you reading your Bible? When you consider that the Bible is a love letter written straight from God's heart to yours, doesn't that make you want to slow down and savor every word? It's the difference between reading the Scriptures and meditating on them. To meditate on something simply means to ponder it, to reflect upon it, or to mull it over in your mind. And when it comes to the Bible, it's not enough simply to read the main idea and let the details disappear in the background. Instead, we should read carefully and intentionally, meditating on God's message in such a way that not a single word falls away. Because when He speaks— Every. Single. Word. Is. Important.

Emily

Garment of praise

To appoint unto them that mourn in Zion,
to give unto them beauty for ashes, the oil of joy for mourning,
the garment of praise for the spirit of heaviness;
that they might be called trees of righteousness,
the planting of the Lord, that he might be glorified.
Isaiah 61:3 KJV

When you are heavy in spirit, hurting, or overwhelmed in any way, this Scripture encourages you to put on "the garment of praise." It's a prescription or cure for those times when you're discouraged and disheartened. The key is in rejoicing, praising God, singing, and worshiping Him—especially during times when you're most prone to feel melancholy or depressed.

Oftentimes, God changes us long before He changes our circumstances. When you put on the garment of praise, He supernaturally enables you to live victoriously above your circumstances.

Laurie

Growing up

*When I was a child, I talked like a child, I thought like a child,
I reasoned like a child. When I became a man,
I put the ways of childhood behind me.*
I Corinthians 13:11 NIV

Your walk with the Lord should become deeper as you grow spiritually. This doesn't necessarily mean that your quiet times should become longer in minutes or more detailed in execution the longer you've been a Christian. It simply means that as you grow, you begin obeying Him more frequently, following Him more regularly and thinking like Him more consistently. You begin maturing.

Emily

At salvation

So you also should consider yourselves to be dead to the power of sin and alive to God through Christ Jesus.
Romans 6:11 NLT

Before you can do anything about the daily spiritual warfare you face, you must first mentally "consider yourself to be dead to the power of sin." In other words, you must believe three things:

- At salvation, you were freed from the penalty of sin.

- At salvation, you were also freed from sin's power.

- And at salvation, you were empowered to new life through the Holy Spirit.

Those are the facts, but knowing them is not enough. Every day you must embrace and believe them as you stand firm in the war against your sinful nature.

Laurie

God-given dreams

"Here comes that dreamer!" they said to each other.
Genesis 37:19 NIV

The Bible does not promote blanket, you-can-have-it-all type dreams that promise health, wealth, and power to any and everyone who "just believes" strongly enough. But God does place dreams in our hearts, and He has the ultimate ability to make those dreams a reality.

Just look at Joseph. When he had a dream as a young child, his dream was big, ridiculous, and made fun of by his entire family. Nevertheless, it came true because it was a God-given dream.

You can let your imagination run wild with ideas of riches, fame and luxury, but God-given dreams do not originate in your imagination. They come from God, settle in your heart, and grow stronger as your relationship with Him grows. The dream God gave Joseph as a young boy had very little to do with Joseph and a whole lot to do with God's plan to save the Israelites from famine years later and to free them from captivity generations later. God makes dreams come true for His benefit, not for yours.

Emily

In training

Physical training is good, but training for godliness is much better,
promising benefits in this life and in the life to come.
I Timothy 4:7 NLT

Just imagine. One of these days, we're going to trade in these aging, achy, gravity-prone bodies for perfect, glorified, heavenly bodies. No more wrinkles, bifocals, diets, exercise, pain, sickness, death and, best of all, no more sin. One sweet day, we will be liberated from the limits and frailties of these earthly tents—our bodies.

But until then, how are we supposed to live in these mortal, physical bodies? If we follow the world's example, it seems we have two choices: (1) we can either worship our bodies by constantly focusing on our quest to fit into Size 2 jeans; or (2) we can destroy our bodies by indulging them in addictive, whatever-makes-you-feel-good behavior.

Neither of those options is good and healthy. But, praise God, there is a much better way. When you gain a biblical perspective about your body, your focus shifts from physical training to training for godliness. And when your focus is on the spiritual, it affects the physical too. You lose many unwanted pounds of worry and self-condemnation, and you may even get a free face lift—it's called a smile—when you focus on how much your Creator loves His original, one-of-a-kind creation—you!

More time

And God is able to bless you abundantly, so that in all things at all times, having all that you need, you will abound in every good work.
2 Corinthians 9:8 NIV

God gives you everything that you need (Phil. 4:19). You've heard this before and you probably remind yourself of this truth whenever you're wishing for more shoes or wanting a bigger house. But have you ever considered that God has also given you all of the *time* that you need as well?

Each day, God gives us 86,400 seconds. Each of us receives the same amount. No more. No less. We are free to spend our seconds as we choose. We can waste them, or we can spend our time wisely. But at the end of the day, we cannot get back those wasted seconds, for they are lost forever.

The God who supplies all of your needs has also given you all of the time that you need as well. How you spend it, however, is up to you.

Emily

Just Jesus

Jesus is "the stone you builders rejected, which has become the cornerstone." Salvation is found in no one else, for there is no other name under heaven given to mankind by which we must be saved.

Acts 4:11-12 NIV

It's easy to get tricked into believing that you have to do something to earn your salvation. I mean, it can't be that easy, can it? Just accept Jesus' sacrifice on the cross and that's it? Surely there's more.

But there's *not* more, and it *is* that easy.

Salvation is not Jesus + [something] or Jesus + [someone]. Salvation is just Jesus. It's not Jesus + [baptism] or Jesus + [perfection] or Jesus + [works]. To suggest that anything else is necessary is to suggest that Jesus couldn't get the job done Himself.

Emily

All nations

All the nations you have made will come and worship before you,
Lord; they will bring glory to your name.
Psalm 86:9 NIV

Today's Psalm is prophetic. It speaks of the time when every nation on earth will give glory to the one true God. Despite today's headlines, despite the current conditions of our world, rejoice in prayer by thanking Him for the glorious future that is ours because He is who He is—God.

Laurie

Messed up?

*Then the women said to Naomi, "Blessed is the Lord
who has not left you without a redeemer today,
and may his name become famous in Israel.
May he also be to you a restorer of life and a sustainer
of your old age; for your daughter-in-law, who loves you and
is better to you than seven sons, has given birth to him."
Then Naomi took the child and laid him in her lap,
and became his nurse.*
Ruth 4:14-16 NASB

Ruth's mother-in-law, Naomi, gives me hope as a woman. She wasn't perfect by any means. She was a woman who messed up, fessed up, yes'ed up, and was blessed up. A flawed woman, behind the scenes, whom God still used in mighty ways.

Even after she blew it with her own sons, God gave her another chance to make a difference. Because she invested in the life of another woman, Ruth, her influence trickled down for generations, forming kings and influencing a nation. Her great-great-grandson, King David, was a man after God's own heart and his son, King Solomon, built the temple of the Lord and was considered the wisest man on earth. Ultimately, her broken road even led to the lineage of Christ.

Have you messed up lately? God can still use you, flaws and all.

Emily

Confession

Then I acknowledged my sin to you and did not cover up my iniquity.
I said, "I will confess my transgressions to the Lord."
And you forgave the guilt of my sin.
Psalm 32:5 NIV

If you would like to enjoy fellowship and intimacy with God, you must seek "clean hands and a pure heart" (Ps. 24:4). You can do this in the same way David did in Psalm 32—through confession and repentance of your sin.

What sin do you need to confess? Read Psalm 32:1-5 to follow David's example and rejoice in God's forgiveness and restored fellowship with Him.

Laurie

His ways are higher

As the heavens are higher than the earth, so are my ways
higher than your ways and my thoughts than your thoughts.
Isaiah 55:9 NIV

At times in my spiritual walk, I find myself expecting and imagining a world in which I can see everything with 20/20 spiritual vision. When I'm going through a difficult time, I imagine that I will come out on the other side with complete understanding as to why God allowed the trial to happen. When God's plan for my life doesn't seem to make sense, I imagine that if I just read the Bible or pray enough, the day will come when all of the pieces will magically come together and I'll suddenly understand His will perfectly. After all, don't they say that hindsight is 20/20?

However, the Bible says that God's ways and thoughts are higher than our own, so it is very possible that His ways may never make sense. The question then becomes, is He still trustworthy even when His ways remain a mystery?

Emily

Copy and shadow

*If [Jesus] were on earth, he would not be a priest, for there are
already priests who offer the gifts prescribed by the law.
They serve at a sanctuary that is a copy and shadow of
what is in heaven. This is why Moses was warned
when he was about to build the tabernacle:
"See to it that you make everything according
to the pattern shown you on the mountain."*
Hebrews 8:4-5 NIV

The tabernacle is an Old Testament type which means it is a
"representation or symbol of something to come."[6] In other
words, it was a copy and a shadow of a future reality. But what
was it a copy and shadow of?

First, the tabernacle symbolizes the church. In Ephesians 2:19-22,
the church is also described as a "holy temple," and as "a
dwelling in which God lives by His Spirit." Secondly, since
1 Corinthians 6:19 says that our "body is the temple of the
Holy Spirit," the tabernacle also symbolizes the individual
believer. Third, the tabernacle represents and symbolizes
heaven, but most importantly, the tabernacle represents and
symbolizes Christ (John 1:14, Heb. 9–10). All throughout the
details of the tabernacle, the future work and person of Christ
are evident.

Laurie

Dragged and enticed

But each one is tempted when, by his own evil desire,
he is dragged away and enticed.
James 1:14 NIV

We should approach the possibility of falling into temptation with the same drive and determination we would use if someone was trying to lock us into the trunk of a car. We would have to be forced into the trunk. We would have to be bound, gagged, and dragged into captivity before we would allow the hood of the trunk to be slammed down on top of us. And once inside, we wouldn't give up and accept defeat. Instead, as soon as the first opportunity to escape presented itself, we would take off running as far and as fast as we could away from our captors.

But many times that's not the case at all. James thought highly of us when he said that we had to be "dragged away and enticed" into sin when all too often, all Satan has to do is suggest we get in the trunk and we hop in voluntarily and close the hood for him.

Don't let that be the case. Instead of lazily falling into temptation, we should fight it! We should run from it! And at the very first chance, we should escape it!

Emily

Embrace the change

Do not conform any longer to the pattern of this world,
but be transformed by the renewing of your mind.
Romans12:2 NIV

Change always leads to choices, and choices are ultimately always made within the heart—which is the primary target for God's chisel of change. Although the changes you are experiencing may be outward—an unexpected move, a child who is struggling, the loss of a job, etc.—God's target is always inward. It's your heart that God really wants to change because only those whose hearts have been changed can truly glorify Him.

Change is essential for salvation (Matt. 18:3), it is a present-tense command to every believer (Rom. 12:2), and it is a future certainty for every Christian (1 Cor. 15:51-52).

The challenge is to embrace the change by praying, "Lord, let the change begin. Change me."

Laurie

God's power and will

*For I have come down from heaven not to do my will
but to do the will of him who sent me.*
John 6:38 NIV

A misconception of God's power comes into play when we perceive that our prayers have gone unanswered. When God chooses *not* to calm the storm, delay death or prevent disaster, it's easy to think, "God didn't do what I wanted Him to do, so that must mean that He can't."

It's not that God can't. It's *never* that He can't. It's just that God has power over Himself too. We call this ability self control, and we usually think of it as something only we need. But God has it too. He has the power to control Himself so perfectly that He never does anything that contradicts His own nature or will.

Emily

Ask for wisdom

Wisdom shouts in the streets.
She cries out in the public square…
Come and listen to my counsel. I'll share
my heart with you and make you wise.
Proverbs 1:20, 23 NLT

Good news! Wisdom is available to everyone who needs it. And we *all* need it. James 1:5 promises that "if any of you lack wisdom, let him ask of God who gives to all men generously and without reproach and it will be given to him" (NASB).

Begin your day by bowing your head and praising God as the source of true wisdom. Ask Him to pour out His wisdom upon you and to make you wise.

Laurie

Any time

*Evening, morning and noon I cry out in distress,
and he hears my voice.*
Psalm 55:17 NIV

What is the best time of day for you to spend time with the Lord? Perhaps it's when your kids and husband have gone off to school and work for the day. Maybe it's fifteen minutes before you begin your work day. Maybe it's during your kids' nap time, or during lunch, or at the end of the day when your house is finally quiet.

There's no "right" time of day to talk with God. He listens just as attentively in the evenings as He does in the mornings. Even Jesus communicated with God at night. He didn't force His life into a legalistic, morning-only ritual. Instead, He saw any time of day as a chance to meet with His Father. Morning, noon or night. He's available.

Emily

Lazy and idle

Brothers and sisters, we urge you to warn those who are lazy.
I Thessalonians 5:14 NLT

The Bible is clear that we should work hard to meet our own needs. Laziness and idleness are not options. "But those who won't care for their relatives, especially those in their own household, have denied the true faith. Such people are worse than unbelievers" (I Tim. 5:8 NLT).

Notice that the Bible says those who "won't," not those who "can't." There is a difference between those who are having trouble making ends meet despite hard work and those who are having difficulties because they are just plain lazy. When someone is doing all she can, but it's still not enough, feel free to help her. But when you see laziness, idleness or a pattern of always having a hand out and never lifting a finger, you should warn that person. Remind her that the Bible teaches us to work hard to provide for our own needs.

Laurie

Not my will

Father, if you are willing, take this cup from me;
yet not my will, but yours be done.
Luke 15:11-13 NIV

Many times, we're hesitant to pray for God's will because we're not yet ready to silence our own desires. We think that if we still have an opinion on the matter, then we're not yet ready to submit.

However, if we look at the context in which Jesus prayed, "Not my will, but yours be done," we can see that He did so *after* crying out to God and expressing His own personal desires over and over again. "Take this cup from me," He prayed. "This isn't what I want. This feels too difficult to endure. Please let there be another way."

Praying for God's will does not mean that you must altogether silence your own desires. It simply means that you express them with the understanding that God's ways are higher than your ways.

Emily

Avoid division

*I appeal to you, dear brothers and sisters, by the authority
of our Lord Jesus Christ, to live in harmony with each other.
Let there be no divisions in the church. Rather, be of one mind,
united in thought and purpose.*
I Corinthians 1:10 NLT

Not all divisions that happen within the church are a result of theological disagreements. Many are simply a result of varying personal preferences on minor aspects of church such as teaching or music styles. Be very careful to avoid judging others if their preferences differ from yours. As long as the essentials are in place in worship services—as long as God is being lifted up and praised and worshiped, as long as Jesus is being exalted, as long as the Word is being proclaimed and the gospel is being taught—the style doesn't matter. It's the substance that does.

Laurie

God's sovereignty

What then shall we say? Is God unjust? Not at all!
For he says to Moses, "I will have mercy on whom I have mercy,
and I will have compassion on whom I have compassion."
Romans 9:14-15 NIV

If God were all-powerful, and that was all, then He could easily become like an evil genie, doing any and everything He wanted just because He could. But because God is also love, He will not do anything that is not motivated by love. His power, therefore, first gets filtered by His love for us.

Because He is also holy, everything He does, thinks, and speaks must be right, good and perfect. So His power also gets filtered through His holiness. Finally, He is omniscient. He knows the intricate details of what is going on in your individual life, the world, eternity, and the spiritual realm. So He is able to take His power and filter it through His knowledge to determine the best way to execute it.

Therefore, absolute power filtered through perfect love, divine holiness, and infinite knowledge results in sovereign execution of power.

Emily

Sorting through a mess

*Let us not become weary in doing good, for at the proper time
we will reap a harvest if we do not give up.*
Galatians 6:9 NIV

I don't know what your past is like. I don't know what kind
of mess you may be in right now. But I do know one thing.
You can't sit around and think everything is going to get better
without doing something. You need to get into God's Word and
you need to let God's people help you.

If you have a mess you need to sort through, there are several
things you can do. First, you may need to seek help from a
Christian counselor. Second, you must immerse yourself in God's
Word and take the pursuit of His truth seriously. Third, become
active in a Bible-believing church and surround yourself with
like-minded people. Fourth, become accountable to someone
godly like a mentor or a small group of Christian women who can
help and encourage you. Finally, you must not give up. Persevere.
If you do the work of sorting through the mess and do not grow
weary in doing good, God's Word promises that you will reap a
harvest in His timing.

Laurie

What's that smell?

Do not put out the Spirit's fire; do not treat prophecies with contempt. Test everything. Hold on to the good. Avoid every kind of evil.
I Thessalonians 5:19-22 NIV

Have you ever been watching a television show, listening to a sermon, or even receiving advice from a friend, when something suddenly "smelled funny" to you about what you just heard? Maybe you couldn't put your finger on it, but something just seemed out of place or not-quite-right, and the thought crossed your mind that maybe you should investigate and verify that in the Bible before you took it as one hundred percent truth. Well as it turns out, those "What's that smell?" moments are there for a reason, and you shouldn't ignore your instincts when your spirit questions something you've heard.

Most of us are not Bible scholars. We have a general foundation of the Scriptures, but not enough to declare ourselves experts in the fields of biblical theology or doctrine. If that's the case, how are we ever to know if what we're taught accurately follows God's Word or not? That's when the "smell test" can come in handy. Many times, the Holy Spirit will prompt our hearts just enough to put a question mark in our minds when we hear something that warrants further investigation. It is our responsibility to investigate the foul odor and see if that message aligns with the Bible or not.

Emily

Glo: 365 Devotions to Give God Priority

may

Behind and before

You have enclosed me behind and before,
and laid Your hand upon me.
Psalm 139:5 NASB

When a child is ready to take his first steps, what do parents tend to do? First they take their child to the den or living room and clear out all of the furniture to protect him if he falls. Then Mom sits on the floor and Dad sits just a few feet away. They become bookends of safety, one behind the child, one before the child, as he teeters with each step between them.

This is exactly what God does for us. First, He takes great care to remove things from our lives that could hurt us should we fall (because we're going to fall). Then He stands behind us, encouraging us to move forward and giving us a gentle nudge when we need it. And He also stands before us, giving us something certain to look to, something worth walking towards and something safe to fall into.

Laurie

A bold, scary prayer

*Search me, God, and know my heart; test me and know
my anxious thoughts. See if there is any offensive way in me,
and lead me in the way everlasting.*
Psalm 139:23-24 NIV

These verses in the book of Psalms don't provide a nice, cozy campground where you want to set up your tent. Instead, they are a little more uncomfortable, an invitation for God to examine you for any area—large, small, insignificant, or secret—to see if there is anywhere that you're not being fully obedient to His Word.

The thought of repeating David's prayer may feel like a recipe for condemnation. But the point of this bold, scary prayer is not so that God can pick you apart, condemn you and criticize you to the point that you feel like a complete failure. The point is so that He can *lead you in the way everlasting*. So that He can fix it!

He does not ask you to pray boldly for a spotlight on your filth without the promise that He can clean it. So, yes, it's a bold, scary prayer. But we have a bold and loving God.

Emily

Open book

Publish His glorious deeds among the nations.
Tell everyone about the amazing things He does.
Psalm 96:3 NLT

Your life is a book that others are reading. Spend a few moments in prayer, and ask God to be glorified through every chapter of the story of your life. Ask Him to give you opportunities today to share with others the amazing things He has done in your life.

Laurie

Be still

Be still and know that I am God.
Psalm 46:10 NLT

We think that being still is difficult for children, but it's difficult for adults too. There's so much to clean. So much to fix. So much to cook. So much to do.

It's good to be productive, but it's also good to "cease striving" (NASB) sometimes too. Today, even if it's just for five minutes, try to practice the art of being still. Don't focus on praying. Don't read. Don't plan your day. Just "Be still and know that I am God."

Emily

The Lord be with you

In everything he did he had great success,
because the Lord was with him.
I Samuel 18:14 NIV

As a leader and warrior, David experienced great personal success as well as innumerable victories in battle. Yes, he was a disciplined leader and a well-prepared warrior, but the primary reason for David's success was that the Lord was with him.

God has given you a flock—maybe it's your children, your friends, your employees, or maybe He's called you to a place of service in your church. But whether you lead sheep or soldiers, you need the Lord to be with you if you want to be successful. Is He directing your steps? Is He guiding your path? Follow His lead in order to lead others.

Laurie

The blessing of work

For we are God's handiwork, created in Christ Jesus to do good works, which God prepared in advance for us to do.
Ephesians 2:10 NIV

The Bible is very clear that the Christian life is not a life of lucrative living and bottomless blessings. We are called to be workers—not to attain our salvation but as a result of our salvation.

However, how many times have we approached God in the same way a child approaches her father? We pray for Him to bless us. We pray to be used in great and mighty ways. Yet, when He asks us to work for what we want, even just a little, we throw our hands up in the air and give up. When it comes right down to it, we don't want to work for our blessings; we just want to be blessed.

God wants to bless you. But He also knows that often the greatest blessings are not in the end result, but in the process of attaining the end result. So when you pray for God to bless you, don't be surprised if He immediately calls you into action.

Emily

Careful thought

Now this is what the Lord Almighty says:
"Give careful thought to your ways."
Haggai 1:5 NIV

The Israelites have the infamous reputation for being more consumed with their own daily lives and their own wellbeing more than they were with putting God first. Many of us follow that same pattern. What are some of the things that vie for first place in your life? What are some of the things that often threaten to consume you? It's not always "bad stuff" that keeps you from putting God first in your life. Often, it's the good stuff in your life that overtakes the best. And the best is seeking Christ first and giving Him priority in your life.

It's time to consider everything—good stuff and bad stuff—that prevents you from giving God first place in your life. Be honest with God about it. And remember, just as He knew the truth about the people of Israel, He knows the truth about you, too. So follow God's advice to the Israelites and, "Give careful thought to your ways."

Laurie

Even in suffering

*To the elders among you, I appeal as a fellow elder
and a witness of Christ's sufferings who also
will share in the glory to be revealed.*
I Peter 5:1 NIV

The Bible mentions three times that Peter tried unsuccessfully to prevent Christ from suffering. Finally, he came to understand that it was Christ's suffering that made it possible for him to share in Christ's glory. But there's more. Peter also came to understand that before we can experience eternal glory, *we* must suffer, too.

Are you suffering today? If so, take comfort from someone who tried—not once, not twice, but three times—to prevent the suffering of Christ. Peter's words, transcribed under the inspiration of the Spirit, were written to remind and encourage you that suffering is the pathway to glory. And you don't want to allow anything to prevent you from glorifying God. So, precious sister, even in suffering, *glo*.

Laurie

Forever friends

Never abandon a friend.
Proverbs 27:10 NLT

It can be a very sad day when you feel as if a friend has "moved on" without you. The girlfriend who used to share your frustrations about dating now doesn't. The friend who used to have time for you is now distracted by her children. The friend who used to be so independent and carefree needs you more and more now that she's a widow.

These situations are real and tough, and sometimes, they are the beginning of a fizzling friendship. But instead of letting that precious friendship fizzle, remember and accept that friendships can, and will, ebb and flow over time. As Michael W. Smith put it so perfectly, "Friends are friends forever if the Lord's the Lord of them."

Emily

Martha's meltdown

*"Yes, Lord," [Martha] told him. "I have always believed
you are the Messiah, the Son of God, the one
who has come into the world from God."*
John 11:27 NLT

Most people are familiar with Martha's meltdown in Luke 10:38-42. Martha complained to Jesus that her sister, Mary, wasn't helping with the housework and Jesus shocked her by saying that, by sitting at His feet, Mary was doing something better than housework.

But we forget about the other side of Martha that is shown in John 11. The side of Martha that appeared after her brother died. The side that was confident in Christ without the slightest hint of a meltdown in the making. Sure, Martha had a meltdown, but she didn't let that define who she was.

You may or may not have a meltdown today. You may or may not whine about your life and have to face reproof by Jesus. But whatever you do, don't allow one meltdown to define who you are.

Laurie

Filthy rags

*All of us have become like one who is unclean, and all our
righteous acts are like filthy rags; we all shrivel up like a leaf,
and like the wind our sins sweep us away.*

Isaiah 64:6 NIV

Sometimes we can get caught up in how we look spiritually as
opposed to those who are not as mature in their faiths, and we
can become pretty confident in our own righteous appearance.
But the Bible says that our righteousness is like "filthy rags," and
that's a truth we sometimes forget when we compare ourselves
to others. Perhaps we tithe more than our neighbors, read our
Bibles more than our coworkers, or volunteer more than some of
our friends. On the surface, we feel great! We may even go so far
as to metaphorically pat ourselves on the back and congratulate
ourselves on how "holy" we have become.

But the day will come when we stand next to the One who truly
is holy, and that's when our own righteousness will be revealed
for what it truly is. Filth. Dirt. Rags. Sin. Next to Christ, there is
no comparison.

Thankfully, all hope is not lost. When Jesus died on the cross,
He exchanged His own royal robes of righteousness for our
filthy rags of sin. And when we accept that marvelous display of
love, our filthiness disappears, and we become the righteousness
of Christ.

Emily

No fear

They were all trying to frighten us, thinking, "Their hands will get too weak for the work, and it will not be completed." But I prayed, "Now strengthen my hands."
Nehemiah 6:9 NIV

Fear did not paralyze Nehemiah, nor did it prevent him from completing the work to which God had called him. He was not intimidated by the discouraging words of his enemies and his faith in God superseded any fear he had of mere men.

Fear continues to be one of Satan's chief weapons of choice as he seeks to intimidate and manipulate you with his threats and accusations. His fear tactics have not changed, nor have His motives. It is exactly as it was in Nehemiah's day. He wants you to become so frightened and discouraged that you abandon the work God has called you to do—the work of glorifying Him and being His witness in a lost and darkened world.

Laurie

Mind-boggling evidence

And all that dwell upon the earth shall worship him,
whose names are not written in the book of life of the Lamb
slain from the foundation of the world.
Revelation 13:8 KJV

It's hard enough to grasp the truth of Romans 5:8, "But God demonstrates his own love for us in this: While we were still sinners, Christ died for us" (NIV). That Jesus would die for us in spite of our sin is mind-boggling.

But what is even more mind-boggling is that before God created man from the dust of the earth, before man willfully chose to sin, God had already provided the remedy for sin. The Bible says that Jesus, the Son of God, the Lamb was "slain from the foundation of the world." What astounding proof and rock-solid evidence of the eternal love and grace of God.

Laurie

Encouraging prayers

I always thank my God as I remember you in my prayers.
Philemon 1:4 NIV

Your prayers are a valuable asset in encouraging others. When someone knows that she is being prayed for, it's like an automatic boost of energy and comfort. When Paul prayed for others, he let them know in the letters he wrote to them:

- *I have not stopped giving thanks for you, remembering you in my prayers* (Eph. 1:16 NIV).

- *In all my prayers for all of you, I always pray with joy* (Phil. 1:4 NIV).

- *We always thank God, the Father of our Lord Jesus Christ, when we pray for you* (Col. 1:3 NIV).

- *We always thank God for all of you and continually mention you in our prayers* (1 Thess. 1:2 NIV).

It's one thing to pray for those you encounter. It's another to tell them that you're praying for them. Who needs to be encouraged with the knowledge that you're praying for them today?

Emily

Road to victory

*For all those who exalt themselves will be humbled,
and those who humble themselves will be exalted.*

Luke 14:11 NIV

Everyone has felt like a victim at one point or another. When we see the ungodly prosper, we feel slighted. When we see evil prevail, even temporarily, we feel forgotten. Feeling like a victim is a sad, helpless, hopeless feeling.

And for Christians, it's completely unfounded.

Part of the problem is that we forget the end of the story. We forget that we win! We forget that Christ reigns! We forget that death leads to life! We forget all of this and focus on what's right in front of us instead. And so we feel like a victim.

But we're anything but! In Christ, we're victors! We're warriors! We're winners and we're conquerors! But, in order to get to that truth, we have to take a very unlikely path:

Humility.

The road to victory is paved with humility. Lay aside your pride. Submit to God. Humble yourself to His will. Only in taking this unlikely path will you finally prevail!

Emily

Build your home

A wise woman builds her home,
but a foolish woman tears it down with her own hands.
Proverbs 14:1 NLT

Wisdom enables us to build our homes and to build up the people we love. Sadly, we have all witnessed the opposite and destructive effect of those who choose to ignore wisdom. Ask God to give you wisdom to build your home, your family, and those you love today.

Laurie

The source of strength

David was now in great danger because all his men were very bitter about losing their sons and daughters, and they began to talk of stoning him. But David found strength in the Lord his God.
1 Samuel 30:6 NLT

In 1 Samuel 30, David and his men suffered a serious setback. They returned to camp to find that the Amalekites had raided their camp and captured all of their women and children. David's men were so distressed, they wanted to stone him.

You may be feeling distressed yourself right now, but it's probably not so bad that someone wants to stone you. Nevertheless, it can feel just as hopeless when you're smack dab in the middle of a hardship, trial, or difficult circumstance. You know the path you're on leads to victory in Christ, but you're tripping over the very stones that pave that path.

"But David found strength in the Lord his God." The only way to get through any difficult circumstance is to remember that your strength comes from God and from Him alone. If you rely on anything or anyone else, you will be let down.

Emily

The importance of prayer

David inquired of the Lord...
1 Samuel 30:8 NIV

After the Amalekites invaded the Israelites and captured their women and children, David didn't know what to do next. He wasn't sure if he should surrender or attack, so he asked the Lord for wisdom.

Often times, the most difficult part of any setback is not knowing what to do next. Your steps may not be clear, or it may seem that the roadblocks in front of you are so big that there aren't even any steps for you to choose from. Ask God for clarity, wisdom, and discernment as to how, when and where to put one foot in front of the other.

Emily

The threat of exhaustion

Two hundred of them were too exhausted to cross the valley...
1 Samuel 30:10 NIV

Even when God is in control, as He was when David led his men to pursue the Amalekites, the possibility of exhaustion is still very real. Exhaustion does not necessarily mean you're on the wrong path. Sometimes it simply means that God wants to do more of the work for you.

Emily

Fight and persevere

David fought them from dusk until the evening of the next day…
I Samuel 30:17 NIV

After the Amalekites captured their women and children, God promised that David and his army would have success in their rescue mission. But the men still had to fight for the victory they had been promised.

Even when God has promised victory, He still requires you to work towards that victory. This is where many people get discouraged because they think that everything should be easy if they're following God. Not true. Sometimes you're in the midst of a battle and you simply must fight.

Not only must you fight, but sometimes you must fight for a long time. David fought from dusk until the evening of the next day. Some battles require weeks of sleepless nights. Some require years of prayer. Some require a lifetime of persistence. Keep fighting and persevere.

Emily

The promise of restoration

David recovered everything the Amalekites had taken…
I Samuel 30:18 NIV

The joy in victory is in the restoration. Sometimes it happens this side of heaven, like it did for David when he fought the Amalekites, and sometimes it doesn't. But with the gift of eternal life and the promise that not even death can separate us from God and His love, the promise of restoration is worth any hardship on the path to victory!

Emily

You can smile

Strength and dignity are her clothing, and she smiles at the future.
Proverbs 31:25 NASB

Even if you have gotten off to a rocky start, there is still hope. Even if you have had a bad beginning, God can still give you a glorious ending. Even during those seasons when you make things messier than they already were, He can change your thought process and give you a new belief system. Even if you are faithless, He remains faithful (2 Tim. 2:13).

God can clothe you with strength and dignity if you will let Him. He can show you how to smile at your future if you will watch Him. He can use you in a very instrumental way if only you will allow Him to take your mess and turn it into a message.

Laurie

Church discipline

Dear brothers and sisters, if another believer is overcome by some sin, you who are godly should gently and humbly help that person back onto the right path. And be careful not to fall into the same temptation yourself.

Galatians 6:1 NLT

The body of Christ is the bride of Christ, and we need to do our part to be a church and a bride that is pure and holy and without blemish. Sometimes that involves church discipline.

The steps of church discipline are outlined in detail in Matthew 18:15-17, but should you have to confront a fellow believer who is caught in sin, the main thing to remember is to do so with humility and gentleness. It helps to remind yourself as you speak to that person, "This could be me. I could be here. This very same thing could happen to me and I could fall into this very same trap of sin."

Never do anything until the Lord clearly shows you that you need to move. Then cast aside any feelings of judgment or self-righteousness and remember that your ultimate goal of repentance and restoration.

Laurie

*Cleanse me with hyssop, and I will be clean; wash me,
and I will be whiter than snow. Let me hear joy and gladness;
let the bones you have crushed rejoice. Hide your face
from my sins and blot out all my iniquity.*
Psalm 51:7-9 NIV

There are only two types of people. Not the good and the bad. But those who repent and those who do not. It's your willingness to repent, not your ability to be good, that draws you closer to God.

David repented of adultery and murder. Peter repented of denying Christ. The thief repented on the cross. The woman in adultery repented at Jesus' feet. Paul repented of persecuting Christians. Hezekiah repented of his pride.

What about you? It's not a matter of if you are good versus if you are bad. (Hint: You're bad. See Romans 3:23). Rather it's a matter of, are you willing to repent or not?

Emily

Because I fear God

But because I feared God, I did not act that way.
Nehemiah 5:15 NLT

The enemy wants us to keep our mouths shut and to abandon the great work of proclaiming the gospel. He uses fear to keep us mute to the freedoms and opportunities we now have in this country, which we may not have much longer if we fail to act upon them. Fear continues to be a powerfully motivating tool Satan uses against the body of Christ.

There is, however, a very different and very positive aspect of fear taught in Scripture. We see that aspect of fear in Nehemiah's life. Because of the fear of God, he was obedient to accomplish God's mission for his life. He did not fear the threats of the enemy. He did not fear the anger and opinions of men. Nehemiah only feared God. And so should we.

Laurie

Spiritual dimension

For our struggle is not against flesh and blood, but against the rulers,
against the authorities, against the powers of this dark world and
against the spiritual forces of evil in the heavenly realms.
Ephesians 6:12 NIV

When we're sitting comfortably on our couches, eating a snack and enjoying Netflix on our high resolution flat screen TVs, it's easy to forget that there is another dimension still at work. The spiritual dimension. The realm of good versus evil where evil so desperately wants to triumph.

But never forget that there is always a spiritual side to every struggle you're facing. It's never just about a fight you're having with your husband. It's never just about your wayward teen. It's never just about what you're watching on TV, reading on your tablet or hearing on your radio.

There's more to it than that. There is a spiritual dimension at work that you may be forgetting. It's warfare and sometimes our couches are the front lines.

Emily

Value in suffering

*And the God of all grace, who called you to his eternal glory in Christ,
after you have suffered a little while, will himself restore you and
make you strong, firm and steadfast.*
1 Peter 5:10 NIV

When Peter woke up on the Mount of Transfiguration and
saw Moses, Elijah, and Jesus in all of their glory, he was
ready to say good-bye to fishing forever and become a full-fledged
mountain man (Luke 9:28-36). He never wanted to leave that
mountain—and who could blame him?

But Jesus knew something Peter didn't. Jesus knew He could
not remain on that mountain. Jesus knew He must descend
from the Mount of Transfiguration so He could ultimately climb
Mount Calvary.

Although Peter didn't realize it, his desire to begin a building
campaign on the Mount of Transfiguration was really just another
attempt to prevent Christ's suffering. It wasn't until after the
resurrection and ascension that Peter fully understood the
necessity of Christ's suffering. Later, when Peter wrote the book
of 1 Peter (a book that's only five chapters long) he used the
word "suffering" over fifteen times. At last he learned that there
is value in suffering.

Laurie

*Now if we are children, then we are heirs—heirs of God
and co-heirs with Christ.*
Romans 8:17 NIV

Do you know who your Father is? Not your earthly father, who may or may not have a vegetable garden. But your Heavenly Father, who has acre upon acre of blessings and promises for you to claim. How well do you really know Him?

Because we are His children, we are also His heirs. But how are we to ever claim our inheritance unless we get to know our Father? Our Father's garden contains anything we could ever need to sustain us in this life. Rows and rows of wisdom are available to us whenever we crave it. Fields of forgiveness stretch past the horizon. And trees of love bear their fruit year-round, with roots so deep they could never be uprooted.

Knowing your Father means knowing the fruit—the promises—He offers to His children.[7]

Emily

A renewed mind

*Make me understand the way of Your precepts,
so I will meditate on Your wonders.*
Psalm 119:27 NASB

God blesses and changes the lives of those (like you) who choose to study His Word. Have you noticed that when you take time to read and study the Bible consistently, you also find yourself thinking about the Word more consistently? This kind of thinking is true, biblical meditation. And consistent meditation results in a renewed mind. And a renewed mind results in a transformed life—hallelujah!

As you think about God's Word, ask Him to allow it to radically renew your mind and to totally transform your life. That's a prayer He's going to want to answer!

Laurie

Meditate day and night

Keep this Book of the Law always on your lips;
meditate on it day and night, so that you
may be careful to do everything written in it.
Then you will be prosperous and successful.
Joshua 1:8 NIV

It's unfortunate that meditation has gotten such a bad reputation in Christian circles because God told us in His Word to meditate long before the New Age movement ever came to be. There are two major differences, however, between traditional forms of meditation and Christian meditation. In traditional forms of meditation, the individual seeks to empty himself; in Christian meditation the believer seeks, rather, to be filled. In traditional meditation, the object is self, albeit the higher self, whereas in Christian meditation the object is God, who is highest above all.

Emily

Glo with the flow

*May the God who gives endurance and encouragement
give you the same attitude of mind toward each other
that Christ Jesus had, so that with one mind and one voice
you may glorify the God and Father of our Lord Jesus Christ.*

Psalm 119:27 NASB

Go with the flow. Now there's a little piece of advice you've heard dozens of times. Usually it just means to do whatever you think is best. Or sometimes it means to do what everyone else thinks is best. And it may even mean that you shouldn't even think about it at all—just let go and go with it, whatever it may be.

Here's a much better saying: *Glo* with the flow. Translation: Glorify God by allowing the Holy Spirit to flow in your life. Going with the flow can get you in a big mess fast! But when you *glo* with the flow, God's Spirit steers you away from messes—He can even get you out of messes that you've already made. So let the Spirit flow, and He'll let your life *glo!*

Laurie

June

When you're interrupted

*When Jesus heard what had happened, he withdrew
by boat privately to a solitary place. Hearing of this,
the crowds followed him on foot from the towns.*
Matthew 14:13 NIV

Imagine how Jesus felt when He heard that John the Baptist had been beheaded. Imagine how His heart hurt and how much He wanted to seek God and be comforted by the Holy Spirit in that moment. But when He tried to get away, the people followed Him, found Him and interrupted His time with His Father before it ever even began.

Has that ever happened to you? Have your intentions ever been interrupted by your responsibilities? If Jesus reacted like we do, we'd expect Him to feel extreme dread and resentment when He arrived on land and to chastise the crowd for following Him on foot. But Jesus didn't chastise the people who needed Him at all. Instead, "When Jesus landed and saw a large crowd, he had compassion on them and healed their sick" (v. 14). He didn't scold them; He healed them. He didn't ignore them; He loved them. And He didn't turn them away so He could feed Himself spiritually. He drew them closer so He could feed them spiritually and physically.

Emily

As soon as possible

After he had dismissed them, he went up
on a mountainside by himself to pray.
Matthew 14:23 NIV

It's important to notice that even though Jesus was interrupted by a crowd of people when He was on His way to spend time with His Father, He still followed through on His original intentions, and so should you.

It's one thing to take care of your responsibilities. But if you're not careful, your days of missed quiet times will turn into weeks, weeks will turn into months, and before long, your seasons of chaos will turn into a lifetime of excuses.

But that won't happen if you do what Jesus did. He got back to His time with the Father as soon as possible. After He was interrupted by the crowd, He spent a whole day caring for them. He ended the evening by taking five loaves of bread and two fish and feeding the entire crowd of more than five thousand people. But as soon as everyone's needs were met and the people left, "He went up on a mountainside by himself to pray."

He may have missed the quiet time He intended to have earlier in the day, but even while He was distracted by a tangent of obligations, He never forgot where His heart was headed. He remained focused on His Father, and when the first window of opportunity opened for Him to return to His original plan for solitude and prayer, He took it.

Emily

All day long

> *O God, we give glory to you all day long*
> *and constantly praise your name.*
> Psalm 44:8 NLT

Are you glorifying God all day long? Even when you're tired? Even when you're running late? Even when you're surrounded by incompetence? To give Him glory a few times a day is wonderful, but it sometimes takes a reminder to glorify Him all day long.

Write the words from this Psalm on a sticky note, and strategically place it where you most need to be reminded of its message—like on your desk at work, or near your kitchen sink where dirty dishes seem to constantly multiply! Begin practicing this Scripture right now by praising and glorifying God in prayer, and don't forget to praise and glorify Him for your job, for dirty dishes and for all of those other daily blessings in disguise.

Laurie

Me party

And be sure of this: I am with you always,
even to the end of the age.
Matthew 28:20 NLT

There's a new pity party in town, and it's called a "Me Party." Basically, it's a pity party wrapped in cute clothes, great food, fun times and, if you're lucky, backup dancers. And the best part of all, it's all about Y-O-U!

The world will tell you that when you have a setback at work, a fight with your husband, a harsh word from a friend or PMS, you deserve a Me Party. Your own Me Party could involve retail therapy, an unnecessarily long bubble bath, an overindulgence of food, alcohol or drugs or simply an escape through a movie, a book, sleep or a random destination.

But the truth is, you're less likely to need a Me Party when every day is a He Party. If you're spending regular, quality time with God, your desire for a Me Party will dissolve. God is with you. He has not left you. He has not forgotten about you. He has not neglected you. He always cares, and He is always working behind the scenes in your life. So you're never truly alone, even at a Me Party.

It's fine to take some time to yourself every now and then, just be careful to keep your Me Party from becoming the social event of the year. It's hard to focus on yourself when you're focusing on Him instead.

Emily

Errands for God

"Go and see how your brothers and the flocks are getting along,"
Jacob said. "Then come back and bring me a report."
So Jacob sent him on his way, and Joseph traveled to
Shechem from their home in the valley of Hebron.
Genesis 37:14 NLT

After that conversation, Joseph ran an errand for his father—and he ended up in Egypt. That errand changed Joseph's life and, ultimately, led him to become the second most powerful man in Egypt. But it wasn't the actual errand that changed Joseph life. It was his obedience. Specifically, his obedience to his father.

Your heavenly Father requires you to run errands for Him, too. He may prompt you to call someone, send an encouraging email, give a needed hug, meet someone's financial need or just spend a few minutes focused solely upon Him. God has a list of errands for you to run. And like Joseph, running errands for God will place you on His amazing path for your life. But you must take the first step and obey.

Laurie

No longer a slave

*But thanks be to God that, though you used to be slaves to sin,
you have come to obey from your heart the pattern of teaching
that has now claimed your allegiance. You have been set free
from sin and have become slaves to righteousness.*
Romans 6:17-18 NIV

When the Egyptians were swallowed by the Red Sea, the threat of slavery did not disappear underwater with the chariots. The threat of slavery followed the Israelites wherever they went. Through Moses, God had delivered them from slavery, yes. But He would continue to deliver them, time after time.

The threat of slavery follows us around as well. We may feel as though, at any minute, sin will attack and we'll be slaves once again to our sinful nature.

But the truth is, if you've accepted Christ, any threat of slavery to sin is simply that—a threat. An empty, shallow, false illusion that Satan waves in your face in order to throw you off track. Just as Joshua conquered Jericho, just as Samson defeated the Philistines and just as David defeated Goliath, Jesus defeated Satan—and sin—on the cross.

Emily

With gladness

Serve the LORD with gladness;
come before Him with joyful singing.
Psalm 100:2 NASB

Does this verse reveal anything about your attitude and service to God? If your motivations are not in check, it can reveal that you are not serving Him the way He wants to be served. Instead of serving Him with gladness, maybe your service to Him is being motivated by guilt, anticipated with dread, or done out of mere obligation.

If you've lost your joy in service, start to reclaim it with joyful singing. God created you to be a beautiful reflection of His glory (1 Cor. 6:19-20). So today, pick up the familiar refrains of Psalm 100 and be beautiful. When you sing, thank, praise and maybe even shout to God with joy, it will be natural to serve Him with gladness once again.

Laurie

Make me clean

Lord, if you are willing, you can make me clean.
Luke 5:12 NIV

It's funny how often we get ourselves into messes without even realizing it. Satan's good like that. It seems that he waits until we're not looking—until we're distracted by the happenings of our lives—and puts something sticky right in our paths. Without fail, we seem to touch it, step in it, or sit in it and walk around foolishly, unaware of our filth. It's so important to look before we sit down, isn't it? To remain alert and aware of our surroundings. Be self-controlled and alert. "Your enemy the devil prowls around like a roaring lion looking for someone to devour" (1 Pet. 5:8 NIV).

Have you stumbled into a messy situation? Don't waste time making excuses for your filth or blaming it on whoever put the mess along your path. Instead, slip away to the foot of the cross, turn on the faucet of God's love, and let Him wash you white as snow.

He is willing. Are you?

Emily

Above your hormones

> But he said to me, "My grace is sufficient for you,
> for my power is made perfect in weakness."
> Therefore I will boast all the more gladly about my
> weaknesses, so that Christ's power may rest on me.
>
> 2 Corinthians 12:9 NIV

Three times, Paul prayed that God would remove the "thorn in his flesh," or the physical infirmity that plagued him. But each time God said, "My gracious favor is all you need."

We suffer from physical infirmities also—they're called hormones! And if you're like most women, you've probably pleaded that God would remove the "crazies" from your life. He's not going to remove that thorn in your flesh, but in those days when your hormones are taking you down emotional roads that you know you don't need to travel, you can choose to respond like Paul did. Paul celebrated his weakness as a chance to tap into God's power. You've got to learn that you are weak, but He is strong. And in your weakness, you can either succumb to the crazies, or you can surrender to the power that is greater than yours and you can learn to live above your hormones. The choice is yours.

Laurie

God's timing

*Now Sarai, Abram's wife, had not been able to bear children for him.
But she had an Egyptian servant named Hagar.*
Genesis 16:1 NLT

Sometimes, submitting to God's timing can be so difficult. I can't help but think about Abraham and Sarah. They wanted to have a child, and God promised that it would happen. But then time passed, and they grew older. And with time came doubt. They began to wonder if they had heard God incorrectly. Maybe He had forgotten about them. Maybe they misunderstood. Maybe they were supposed to help God out a little.

They had submitted to His will; they just hadn't submitted to His timing.

Many times we'll give God a certain time limit, and if He doesn't move within those parameters, we assume He's not going to move at all. When you pray for God's timing, don't put conditions on waiting, and don't hang your personal clock on the wall next to God's and compare time zones.

Emily

Self-love

*Jesus replied: "'Love the Lord your God
with all your heart and with all your soul and
with all your mind.' This is the first and greatest
commandment. And the second is like it:
'Love your neighbor as yourself.'"*
Matthew 22:37-39 NIV

One of the main things that keeps us from loving God and loving others the way that Jesus commands is the distraction of self. Self-love in particular is an epidemic in today's society, but it's a battle we've been fighting ever since Adam and Eve sinned in the garden.

One of the main ways we see self-love is through our conversation skills. Ask yourself if you're the one doing all the talking. Is your conversation all about you or are you asking questions and listening well? When you constantly think about self, talk about self and put yourself first, you are doing the opposite of loving God and loving others. It is impossible to glorify God if self is on the throne.

Laurie

God knows

*O Lord, you have examined my heart and
know everything about me.*
Psalm 139:1 NLT

God is omniscient, or more simply, He is all-knowing. His knowledge is not limited by time, space or darkness. And He doesn't have to process His thoughts in order to comprehend them; He just knows.

Depending on your relationship with God, His omniscience is either a blessing or a bother. For most, it comes as a sweet sigh of relief. God knows you. He knows you even better than you know yourself. He knows your day dreams and your nightmares. He knows what you worry about. He knows how much you love your family. He knows what you need and what you want. He knows how fragile you are and how strong you can be.

Omniscient is a big word. But it simply means that He knows your heart, He sees the future, and He has all the answers.

Emily

Transformed

Do not conform to the pattern of this world,
but be transformed by the renewing of your mind.
Romans 12:2 NIV

The life Christ died to give us is joyful, meaningful, and deeply satisfying because He satisfies. The question we should ask ourselves then is, "Is my Master satisfied with me?"

The Bible is God's perfect mirror, and it reveals something about you every time you look into it. What did you see when you looked into God's mirror yesterday? But even more importantly, what do you see now? God's Word is immutable—it does not change. We, on the other hand, are commanded to change and to be transformed. When you allow Him to change and transform you, you will find true and lasting satisfaction in Him, and He will be satisfied with you.

Laurie

Flesh and blood

Because God's children are human beings—made of flesh and blood—the Son also became flesh and blood. For only as a human being could he die, and only by dying could he break the power of the devil, who had the power of death... Therefore, it was necessary for him to be made in every respect like us, his brothers and sisters, so that he could be our merciful and faithful High Priest before God. Then he could offer a sacrifice that would take away the sins of the people. Since he himself has gone through suffering and testing, he is able to help us when we are being tested.
Hebrews 2:14, 17-18 NLT

It's easy to forget about the flesh and blood connection Jesus shares with us. Not the flesh and blood, dying on the cross for our sins part, but the flesh and blood "made in every respect like us...so that he could be our merciful and faithful High Priest" part. The part that made Jesus "able to help us when we are being tested" part. Do you ever forget that?

Satan encourages this forgetfulness by relentlessly reminding you of every failure of your flesh and blood life. And the fallout is that you become so focused upon your failings that you forget the part about Jesus that can help you when you're being tested.

You will face many trials and tests in your flesh and blood life, and you have an enemy who wants to keep you in a state of spiritual amnesia. But do not forget: Because He lived a flesh and blood life, Jesus not only understands every temptation, every fear, every sorrow, every weakness, every circumstance—everything—you will think, feel, and experience, He can also help you through them.

Emily

Sing for joy

The Lord is my strength and my shield;
my heart trusts in him, and he helps me.
My heart leaps for joy, and with my song I praise him.
Psalm 28:7 NIV

So often when we go through trying times, we pray that God will "fix it." Maybe we want a rewind button or a fast forward button so we can skip past the funk or return to better days. But God is not in the business of undoing anything.

Instead, we should pray to see our circumstances through His eyes. Our blessings rather than our trials. The eternal rather than the temporal. His sovereignty rather than His mystery. Comfort does not come in skipping over the grief. It comes in being carried through it. Only then can you sing for joy, even in grief.

Emily

Pray for the workers

*Jesus went through all the towns and villages,
teaching in their synagogues, proclaiming the good news
of the kingdom and healing every disease and sickness.
When he saw the crowds, he had compassion on them,
because they were harassed and helpless, like sheep
without a shepherd. Then he said to his disciples,
"The harvest is plentiful but the workers are few.
Ask the Lord of the harvest, therefore,
to send out workers into his harvest field."*
Matthew 9:35-38 NIV

Do you ever feel helpless when you watch the evening news? Does your heart break for those who are hurting? Do you wish that there was something you could do personally to give hope to those who are in desperate situations?

Jesus and His disciples saw a lot of hurt and a lot of needs as they traveled from town to town teaching. Jesus acknowledged the needs, but He never expected His disciples to personally meet every need they saw. Instead, He told them to pray that God would send others to work the fields where the harvest was plentiful.

When you see tragedy on the news, pray that the Christians and the local churches will rise up and influence those in their communities who are hurting, vulnerable, and in need of God's hope. When you can't reach them personally, pray for the workers who can.

Emily

No longer slaves

If we say we have no sin,
we are deceiving ourselves, and the truth is not in us.
1 John 1:8 NASB

True salvation results in immediate change, progressive change and future change. At salvation, we were freed from the penalty of sin, which is death and separation from God. This is called justification. At salvation, we were also freed from the power of sin through the baptism/indwelling of the Holy Spirit so that we are no longer slaves of sin. This is called sanctification. In the future (when our mortal bodies die and we are with Christ in heaven), we will be freed from the very presence of sin, and we will receive eternal life with Christ and new bodies that cannot sin. This is called glorification.

Therefore, as a Christian, you are justified, you *are being* sanctified, and you *will be* glorified. Justification is a past, completed act in the life of the Christian. Sanctification is an ongoing work within the life of the Christian. Glorification is the future reality for all Christians. But remember, the evidence of true salvation is a changed life, not a perfect life.

Laurie

Truthful lips

*Truthful lips endure forever,
but a lying tongue lasts only a moment.*
Proverbs 12:19 NIV

Are honesty and integrity among the virtues for which you're known by those close to you? What about by God? Does He, who sees all and knows all, also see the truth in you?

The Bible says that the devil is the "father of lies" and that when he lies, he "speaks his native language" (John 8:44 NIV). Most of us don't consider ourselves to be liars about the "big" things in life. We are faithful to our spouses. We don't shoplift. We don't cheat in school. But when it comes to the "little" things, the temptation to fudge the truth is one we face every day, and sometimes, our half-truths and omitted facts seem so insignificant, we don't even realize that it's equivalent to lying.

Unfortunately, a little deception is almost expected these days. People who have already graduated from college still use their student IDs to get discounted movie tickets. Parents lie about their children's ages to avoid paying for their meals at restaurants. Business owners save receipts for personal expenses in order to write them off on their taxes. Small and seemingly "innocent" lies show up so often that most have come to tolerate them and shrug them off as something everyone does anyway.

As Christians, we're to be honest in each and every circumstance— those that are in public, those that are in private, those that seem "big," and those that seem "small."

Emily

Keep pure

Wisdom will save you from the immoral woman,
from the seductive words of the promiscuous woman.
Proverbs 2:16 NLT

Start your day by asking God to search your heart and reveal all the impurities in your life. Be still. Allow God to speak to you. Take time to confess each sin to Him, and receive His cleansing and forgiveness. Commit to complete repentance, and ask God for wisdom to keep you pure.

Laurie

Two will become one

*"Haven't you read," [Jesus] replied, "that at the beginning
the Creator 'made them male and female,' and said,
'For this reason a man will leave his father and mother
and be united to his wife, and the two will become one flesh'?
So they are no longer two, but one flesh. Therefore
what God has joined together, let no one separate."*
Matthew 19:4-6 NIV

When a group of Pharisees asked Jesus, "Is it lawful for a man to divorce his wife for any and every reason?" (Matt. 19:3 NIV), Jesus affirmed the importance of sexuality and oneness in marriage with His response. He not only upheld the sexual relationship of marriage, He hallowed it and made it sacred. While the world debases, dishonors, and degrades sex, God's Word glorifies and upholds it as an act of holiness to be enjoyed and shared by a husband and wife.

Laurie

Open rebuke

> *Better is open rebuke than hidden love.*
> *Wounds from a friend can be trusted,*
> *but an enemy multiplies kisses.*
> Proverbs 27:5-6 NIV

Nothing is more valuable than a friend who will tell you when you have a long line of toilet paper attached to your shoe. Or when you've sat on a brownie and gotten chocolate all over your pants. Or when you're walking around, covered in sin, and don't even know it—or more sadly, don't even care.

Do you know someone who is in a mess and doesn't know it? Be a true friend and reveal to that person, in love, that she's sat on a brownie. Remind her of the forgiving blood of Christ and help her become clean again.

Emily

De-clutter

*Whatever you have learned or received or
heard from me, or seen in me—put it into practice.
And the God of peace will be with you.*
Philippians 4:9 NIV

Are you doing the work necessary to keep your life spiritually clutter-free? Are you intentional about growing and moving forward so that you can keep from turning backwards? Are you taking what you know to be true and putting it into practice?

You may need to make major adjustments in your life in order to apply what you've learned. If so, don't hesitate to get rid of anything that clutters your life and keeps you from focusing on Christ. Find a biblical passage that speaks to you or a biblical role model to emulate in order to reinforce what God is teaching you.

Finally, give back. Use what God has taught you to help others de-clutter their own lives.

Laurie

Puzzling reflections

Now we see things imperfectly,
like puzzling reflections in a mirror,
but then we will see everything with perfect clarity.
All that I know now is partial and incomplete,
but then I will know everything completely,
just as God now knows me completely.
1 Corinthians 13:12 NLT

You may not understand why God did not do something even though you know He could have (like stop a hurricane, heal your cancer, or prevent a disaster). On the surface, it may even feel that if He cared, He would have acted.

But rest assured, the exact opposite is true. You may not see how He's working now. But someday, even if it's not until you're in heaven, you will see and understand. Imagine standing before Him and being able to smile as you say, "Oh! So *that's* why!"

Emily

The heavens proclaim

*The heavens proclaim the glory of God. The skies display
his craftsmanship. Day after day they continue to speak;
night after night they make him known. They speak without
a sound or word; their voice is never heard. Yet their message
has gone throughout the earth, and their words to all the world.*
Psalm 19:1-4 NLT

In the city, we see only the moon and a very small smattering
of stars at night. The glare from man-made lights prevents us
from enjoying the panorama of countless numbers of heavenly
lights. In my own life, it grieves me to say, I see a parallel truth.
At times the glare from my own self glory prevents God's glory
from clearly shining forth through me.

Thankfully, there is a power source that God has placed within
each one of us that removes the glare of sin and self from
our lives and enables us to reflect His light and His glory.
That power source is the Holy Spirit. Today, commit to join the
heavens in declaring the glory of God so that when He tilts His
head toward us and looks upon this dark, sinful world, He will
see far more than just a small smattering of light upon the earth.
Pray that God will see nothing less than a spectacular, glorious
view when He looks our way so that the whole earth will be filled
with His glory (Ps. 72:19)!

Laurie

Signal with your feet

A worthless person, a wicked man,
is the one who… signals with his feet…
Proverbs 6:12-13 NASB

You can often recognize when a person is trying to escape a meeting because his feet will start pointing towards an open door. The body language of the feet very often reflects the true state of a person's mind. But we should not be fooled. God, the creator of the body, can also read body language. He knows when you signal with your feet. He hears your toe tapping in the middle of a long sermon in your vain attempt to speed up the preacher so you can be the first one out the door. He notices the way you slide your feet back and forth as you subconsciously try to map out an escape route to flee a convicting conversation with a spiritual mentor. And, He is saddened when you begin the backwards shuffle away from Him just as the main point of His impromptu meeting with you approaches.

Today become aware of the direction of your feet. When the Lord blesses you with His presence in an impromptu meeting, whether it be via a verse you read in the Bible, a lesson you hear in church, or a convicting thought that enters your mind, take advantage of that time for optimum communication with Him. The Lord often speaks to us during impromptu meetings, and it would be a shame to tap, slide, or shuffle away before we've heard what He has to say.

Emily

Don't be a stumbling block

*And when you sin against other believers by
encouraging them to do something they believe is wrong,
you are sinning against Christ. So if what I eat causes
another believer to sin, I will never eat meat again as long as
I live—for I don't want to cause another believer to stumble.*
I Corinthians 8:12-13 NLT

In the church of Corinth, a lot of people were new believers who formerly worshiped pagan idols. They would take choice cuts of meat and put it at the feet of idols as offerings. But before it spoiled, people would take the meat and sell it and Christians would buy it knowing they had freedom in Christ about what they ate.

New Corinthian believers had a hard time understanding why it was okay to eat meat that had been sacrificed to idols. To them, it was a stumbling block in their new faith and caused them to sin. Paul was very careful to avoid doing anything at all that would cause new believers to sin, so he was willing to place his love of others above his liberties in Christ.

Laurie

Spiritual cleavage

Stand firm then…
with the breastplate of righteousness in place.
Ephesians 6:14 NIV

When it comes to the breastplate of righteousness, most Christians want to wear it more like a push up bra than like a bulletproof vest. They want just enough righteousness to cover "the girls" or to cover their soul and their heart, but not so much that it covers and influences all areas of their morality. They want a breastplate of righteousness that allows for a little spiritual cleavage on the side.

Emily

Self-importance

The greatest among you will be your servant.
For those who exalt themselves will be humbled,
and those who humble themselves will be exalted.
Matthew 23:11-12 NIV

Do you often feel the urge to name-drop? Do you long for that special title after your name? That notable position? That moment of recognition? If so, you may be suffering from the deadly sin of self-importance.

Self-importance is the choice to do good so that you will look good. It's main motivation is to appear important in the eyes of others. If you want to be like Christ and glorify God, you first need to get over yourself. Jesus had a position of authority—He was Lord!—but He chose to be a servant instead of a dictator. Likewise, the only way to be the type of woman that God wants you to be is to be a servant.

Laurie

Time to reevaluate

Do not love the world or anything in the world.
1 John 2:15 NIV

One of Satan's greatest tricks is to distract you with good things. Things like your family members, your productive schedule, celebrations or church activities. All of those things are wonderful blessings from the Lord, but even blessings can become distractions.

It's easy to see when something bad is causing you to drift away from the Lord, but it's harder to notice when it's something good. However, when the good things in your life begin to take priority over the best thing, your relationship with God, it's time to stop and reevaluate.

Emily

Mighty warrior

> *But the Lord is with me like a mighty warrior;*
> *so my persecutors will stumble and not prevail.*
> Jeremiah 20:11 NIV

The prophet Jeremiah obediently delivered God's message to the dull, callous ears of Israel prior to their captivity in Babylon. His message was received with contempt and rage. As a result, Jeremiah was chained and beaten by his own people. Jeremiah 20:7–10 recounts his lament and complaint to God regarding the rejection and reproach he faced from those who had once been his friends

In verse 11, however, we see beyond Jeremiah's tears as he expresses his deep and abiding faith in God. If you are at a place where you feel totally alone and without a Godsend, or if you are at a place where all you can see are the enormous giants threatening to destroy you, claim these words penned by Jeremiah and inspired by God, our steadfast champion.

Take heart and be encouraged. Your God—who is a mighty warrior and a steadfast champion—is standing with you. Believe it!

Laurie

july

The secret to happiness

"I, your Lord and Teacher, have just washed your feet.
You, then, should wash one another's feet...
Now that you know this truth, how happy
you will be if you put it into practice!"
John 13:14, 17 GNT

Happy-go-lucky. Happy birthday. Happily ever after. Happy hour. A happy medium. Happy Days. A happy meal. And, for the *Duck Dynasty* fans, happy, happy, happy!

The word might as well be a magnet because we're all attracted to the idea of being happy! We all want the secret formula, special location or genetic makeup that guarantees, or at least occasionally offers, happiness.

When Jesus washed His disciples' feet in the upper room during the Last Supper, He gave them the secret to happiness. He showed them, by example, how to serve each other. Then He promised that if they did serve each other, they would be happy.

It turns out that the secret to happiness is no secret at all. Happiness is simply found in serving others. So, are you serving others today? I suggest that you give it a try. Do something special for a friend. Surprise your spouse. Help a stranger. Turn your focus away from your funk and focus on the needs of others and see if happiness doesn't follow.

Emily

In good company

*Through their faith, the people in days of old
earned a good reputation.*
Hebrews 11:2 NLT

The eleventh chapter of Hebrews is known as the "Faith Chapter" of the Bible because it lists men and women who, "by faith," did amazing things for the Lord. But though these people stand as pillars of the faith with their godly reputations, it is important to remember that, to the world, they had very different reputations. They appeared to be fools to those who did not understand God's ways, and the Bible says that "the world was not worthy of them" (v. 38 NIV).

Have you ever been in a situation where God called you to do something and you thought, "No way! If I do that, I'll look like an idiot!"? If you have, I want you to know you're in good, good company. The world may say, "That's foolish! That doesn't make sense." But the Christian life is backwards from the way the world is. God sometimes calls us to be a fool for His sake.

Laurie

Real freedom

*I will walk in freedom,
for I have devoted myself to your commandments.*
Psalm 119:45 NLT

Many times we think that if we just had a few days free from our endless responsibilities, we could finally feel rested. But, have you ever spent several days or weeks doing exactly what you wanted only to realize that you still don't feel rested or renewed? You know what? Freedom—real freedom—isn't just doing or not doing what you want, even if it's spending two days vegging out in front of the TV. Freedom is what you get when you get into God's Word. It's the freedom David described in Psalm 119.

Before your day spirals into a blur, and before another week of "freedom" comes and goes, get back into your old routine. Get into God's Word today. And discover that you will never be more free than when you experience R&R God's way!

Laurie

Declaration of dependence

Trust God from the bottom of your heart;
don't try to figure out everything on your own.
Listen for God's voice in everything you do, everywhere you go;
he's the one who will keep you on track.
Proverbs 3:5-6 MSG

Today may be Independence Day, but these days independence is something worthy of celebration *every* day—especially if you're celebrating being an "independent woman." Once you have achieved "independent woman" status, you have truly arrived.

However, to be truly independent means that you are not influenced by the thoughts or actions of others. The very thing that makes independence what it is is that it stands alone and has no outside variables to factor into the equation. Only if you lived in a bubble could you be truly independent because other people interfere with your life every day.

So while the world may tell you that independence is the ultimate goal, the goal that provides the most freedom of all is not independence but dependence on God. Today, instead of focusing on independence, celebrate the day with a "Declaration of Dependence." Allow God to keep you on track and let independence go up with the fireworks.

Emily

July 5

The truth about you

*There is therefore now no condemnation
for those who are in Christ Jesus.*
Romans 8:1 NASB

Do you know who you really are? It is absolutely imperative that you do. Why? Because Satan *does* know the truth about you, and he's totally committed to keeping you from that truth. He wants you to feel condemned, insecure, worthless, and unloved, and he'll use any lie he can think of to make you forget who you are in Christ.

Because the truth is that you are not condemned. You are free, forgiven, valuable and deeply loved. So if you're sick of the lies, arm yourself with God's Word and defeat the false accusations with the truth about who you really are.

Laurie

Fishers of men

And [Jesus] said to them, "Follow Me,
and I will make you fishers of men."
Matthew 4:19 NASB

Several of Jesus' disciples were fishermen by trade before they left their boats to follow Jesus, and when He first met Peter and Andrew, He told them to follow Him and He would make them "fishers of men." They took this call to evangelism seriously as they shared the good news of the gospel everywhere they went, and it's a call to evangelism we still take to heart even today. We're to share Christ with those around us. We're to give our testimonies often. We're to do everything we can to witness to others and be "fishers of men."

But the one thing we so often forget is that God never tells us to be "catchers" of men at all. He just tells us to fish. The burden of the catch has always been on His shoulders, not ours. Sometimes it can take so much preparation to finally build up enough courage to share Christ with someone that we're disappointed if they don't accept Him on the spot. We think maybe we said the wrong thing or we failed in our efforts. But we never know what's going on in a person's heart like God does. And because of that, all we can do is continue to fish—continue to share Christ whenever we can—and leave the catching up to Him.

Emily

Do not delay

I will hasten and not delay to obey your commands.
Psalm 119:60 NIV

Ask God to reveal any areas in your life where you are hesitating to obey Him. It may be fear, pride, or a sin that continually defeats you. It may also be a step of faith He is clearly leading you to take, even though you are unsure of the consequences. Is there any hesitancy in your obedience to Him? If so, confess and repent of it today. Then quickly and without delay, fully obey Him.

Laurie

Well done

> *His master replied, "Well done, good and faithful*
> *servant! You have been faithful with a few things;*
> *I will put you in charge of many things.*
> *Come and share your master's happiness!"*
> Matthew 25:23 NIV

In the Parable of the Talents (Matt. 25:14-30), Jesus tells about three different workers who each received different amounts of money to invest while their master was away. Most people focus on the last worker, the lazy one, who buried his talent and didn't do anything with it. But there is a valuable lesson in the first two workers as well. Even though the first worker ended up with ten talents and the second worker with only four, they were both praised because they did the best with what they had.

Your job may not seem as exciting as the CEO's, and your resources may not be as extravagant, but you can still do a great job with what you have and where you are now!

Emily

A little less talk

Make it your goal to live a quiet life,
minding your own business and working with your hands,
just as we instructed you before.
I Thessalonians 4:11 NLT

You can often spot those who need a lot of attention by how much they talk. They talk and talk and talk—on their cell phones, to their co-workers, to their friends, and to just about anybody who will listen. Their life is anything but quiet and they mind everyone's business but their own. They tell everybody everything and if you tell them something, they'll tell everybody everything about you, too. As a result, their homes are usually a wreck and their performance at work suffers.

Wise women do not monopolize the time and attention of others. They enjoy good conversations, but they are wise and discreet with their words and they know that "too much talk leads to sin" (Prov. 10:19 NLT). Hard-working and productive both at home and at work, it's no wonder these wise women can "smile at the future" (Prov. 31:25 NASB).

Laurie

Little by little

*I will send terror ahead of you to drive out the Hivites, Canaanites,
and Hittites. But I will not drive them out in a single year, because
the land would become desolate and the wild animals would multiply
and threaten you. I will drive them out a little at a time until your
population has increased enough to take possession of the land.*
Exodus 23:28-30 NLT

Even though God promised the Promise Land to the Israelites,
He didn't give it to them right away. They had to wait through
generations of wars, battles, bloodshed and trials before they
were able to take claim of the land that God promised so long
ago. Did God have something to prove? Did He enjoy making the
Israelites wait and work for so long?

Of course not. God had a reason for taking His time, and it turns
out, it makes a lot of sense. If God had given the Israelites all that
He had for them all at once, it would have been too much for
them to handle. The land would have dried up. The animals would
have grown too numerous. There would not have been enough
people to handle their blessings.

So instead, He got rid of their enemies little by little.

Little by little.

It can be hard to wait on God when He's moving "little by little"
and you're wanting "all at once." Sometimes we can misinterpret
God's lack of speed for apathy. But God sees the benefits of time.
He knows that sometimes we need a little extra time to be ready
to handle the blessings that He has in store for us.

Emily

Fashion statement

Make sacred garments for Aaron that are glorious
and beautiful. Instruct all the skilled craftsmen
whom I have filled with the spirit of wisdom.
Have them make garments for Aaron that will
distinguish him as a priest set apart for my service.
Exodus 28:2–3 NLT

The clothing that God commanded for the priests in the Old Testament set them apart and signified the holiness, dignity and honor befitting one called by God to be a priest. God has also called us to be holy and to be priests (1 Pet. 1:15, 2:5). As such, our clothing should reflect holiness, dignity and honor. "Therefore, as God's chosen people, holy and dearly loved, clothe yourselves with compassion, kindness, humility, gentleness and patience. Bear with each other and forgive one another if any of you has a grievance against someone. Forgive as the Lord forgave you. And over all these virtues put on love, which binds them all together in perfect unity" (Col. 3:12-14 NIV).

There's a reason why God is so specific with His recommendations for your moral "garments." He wants you to make a fashion statement like no other!

Laurie

Your unique tool

He replied, "I know nothing about that one way or the other.
But I know one thing for sure: I was blind . . . I now see."
John 9:25 MSG

In John 9, John tells the story of a man who was born blind. Jesus healed him and after he received his sight, others asked him to explain what had happened. The man didn't have all the answers. He wasn't eloquent, and he couldn't explain exactly how Jesus healed him or where Jesus received His power. All he could do was tell them, in very simple terms, his story. "I can't explain what happened! All I can tell you is that I was blind, but now I can see!"

Your personal testimony is one of the greatest tools you have to share Christ with others. It's unique. It's authentic. And it's powerful. You don't have to have all the answers; just tell your story and watch how God is glorified through it!

Emily

Everything on earth

Everything on earth will worship You;
they will sing Your praises, shouting
Your name in glorious songs.
Psalm 66:4 NLT

Over two thousand years ago, Jesus came to the earth as the Lamb of God who was slain for the sins of the world. The Scriptures teach that the second coming of Christ will immediately follow the seven-year period of tribulation and will usher in the millennial reign of Christ. When He returns, He will come as the Lion of Judah, and for 1,000 years, the glory of God's visible, literal presence will dwell upon the earth. It will be a time unlike any era before it.

Can you even imagine what that will be like when today's Psalm is a reality? He will reign. Glory, glory!

Laurie

Hindsight

*But God sent me ahead of you to preserve for you a remnant
on earth and to save your lives by a great deliverance.*
Genesis 45:7 NIV

Joseph's jealous brothers sold him into slavery, and decades later, he was in a position of authority to help them and all of Egypt through a famine. After you know the whole story, it sounds wonderful. But I'm sure Joseph asked, "Why?" before he had the benefit of hindsight. He didn't know that God allowed him to be sold into slavery now so that he could be in a position of authority later, and he couldn't see that everything that looked like a problem on the surface was actually creating a platform that Joseph could use later.

Times will come when things appear as if they're falling apart. Things don't make sense and God seems to be ignoring your cries for help. Like when Moses was pushed into the Nile by his mother, or when Paul was imprisoned, or when Jesus was crucified. You may lose your job, lose your husband, lose your home or lose your health, but when you pray, you begin to see that today's problems might actually be tomorrow's platform.

God has a reason for everything He does. You may not understand. It may not make sense. And you might not always like it at the time. But rest assured that His reasons are divine. And when you know that you can thank Him for it in hindsight, it becomes easier for you to trust Him in the present.

Emily

Behind the cameras

> *Would not God find this out?*
> *For He knows the secrets of the heart.*
> Psalm 44:21 NASB

As a Christian, your deeds are supposed to authenticate the sincerity and genuineness of your faith. Sitting in church wearing your Sunday best, you may appear to be the real deal—a model Christian. The reality, however, of your faith and commitment to Christ will be proven inside your home, at your job, or as you sit alone surfing the Internet.

It's easy to shake your fingers and cluck your tongue at those whose sin and hypocrisy are made public. But what would cameras expose if they were focused on you? If they came into your home, what would they see? If they recorded the conversations you have with your spouse and your children, what would they reveal? If they followed you to your workplace, as you run your errands, or go on a business trip, what would they witness? If they did an in-depth investigation into the entertainment you watch, the videos you rent, the websites you visit, what would they discover?

Laurie

Overlook offenses

A person's wisdom yields patience;
it is to one's glory to overlook an offense.
Proverbs 19:11 NIV

One of the greatest things about how God designed women is that He made us to be sensitive. Sympathy and empathy often come easily to us; our hearts burst during simple moments of blessing, and we care deeply about the inner workings of others. However, one of the greatest challenges about how God designed women is also that He made us to be sensitive. Because our hearts are soft and we care so much what others think, we can sometimes be easily hurt and offended.

You cannot control the thoughts, words and actions of others. But you can control how you react to them. The Bible says to overlook offenses, forgive transgressions and ignore insults. When you choose to respond in this way, you glorify God with the respect and honor you receive.

Emily

Reunion

And if I go and prepare a place for you, I will come back and take you to be with me that you also may be where I am.
John 14:3 NIV

If you've ever lost a loved one, you understand the deep longing to be reunited with those who have passed on. It is a desire so deep, you cannot escape it. So strong, you cannot ignore it. But so personal, you cannot express it. It is a desire of your mind, your heart, and your soul all at once.

The desire for a reunion.

As Jesus prepared to go to the Cross, He addressed this desire and gave His disciples one of the most valuable promises of all time. The promise of a reunion! A reunion that we're invited to as well!

This promise of a reunion is one that grows stronger every time we're bombarded with the darkness of this world and we wish that we could just climb up into Jesus' lap and let Him make it all better. That day is coming. It's a promise that grows sweeter every time you attend a funeral and wish for just one more day, one more conversation or one more kiss. That day is coming. And it's a promise that grows more and more personal every time you look at old photos. Every time you mark another anniversary. Every time you notice that another year has gone by and the desire hasn't gone away. Every time you realize that time doesn't make it easier, it just makes you anticipate heaven that much more. That day is coming!

Praise God! That day is coming!

Emily

Empty promises

"I will give you the glory of these kingdoms and authority over them,"
the devil said, "because they are mine to give to anyone I please."
Luke 4:6 NLT

Satan surely knows how to make empty promises, doesn't he? He promised Jesus, the creator and ruler of the world, that he would give Him glory and authority over all the kingdoms.

Satan's tactics haven't changed through the centuries. He still tries to lure you in by making all kinds of promises that he cannot fulfill. In your own life—in recent days or in the past—how has Satan tempted you by promising to give you glory and authority? What are you doing to remind yourself that his promises are empty promises?

Laurie

Not an entertainer

Even after Jesus had performed so many signs in their presence,
they still would not believe in him.
John 12:37 NIV

God is not in the business of working miracles for entertainment purposes. He doesn't want to impress us; He wants to change us. His goal is to bring Himself glory so that we may know Him, serve Him, and worship Him.

When you see the sick healed, the hungry fed or the lost found, remember that every miracle is merely a means to an end. God does not want to entertain us with His signs and wonders; He wants His signs and wonders to lead us into a deeper relationship with Him.

Emily

Welcome His presence

*The ark of God remained with the family of Obed-Edom
in his house for three months, and the Lord blessed
his household and everything he had.*
1 Chronicles 13:14 NIV

After Uzzah died because he tried to steady the ark of the covenant when it slipped from its new cart, the Israelites' celebration parade came to a screeching halt (see 1 Chron. 13) I imagine everyone started backing away very slowly from the Cadillac cart and the killer ark. As the crowd parted, I envision everyone quietly and cautiously turning their heads in unison to see the response of one man: David. Looking at him, they probably wondered, "What's he gonna do now?" But their very next thought was probably, "I hope David doesn't ask me to help with that killer ark."

Eventually a decision was made. The ark would be taken to Obed-Edom's house. And then a marvelous and almost miraculous thing happened: Obed-Edom willingly received the ark into his home and agreed to become its caretaker. Would you have done that? Surely Obed-Edom was aware of the circumstances of the killer ark and of Uzzah's death. He may have even witnessed it. You won't find very much information about Obed-Edom in the Bible. Yet even the minuscule amount of information we do know about him speaks volumes. The tiny tidbits of knowledge we possess about him simplifies and even emphasizes one single, supernatural truth: Those who willingly welcome the presence of God into their lives will be blessed.

Laurie

Pleasing aroma

*For we are to God the pleasing aroma of Christ among
those who are being saved and those who are perishing.*
2 Corinthians 2:15 NIV

When you smell baby powder, does your mind bring you back
to those middle-of-the-night feedings when your child was
a newborn? When you smell freshly-sharpened pencils, do you
remember your first day of school? What Christmas memories
come to mind when you smell cinnamon or apple cider?

Many studies prove that our memories are triggered by smells
more so than any other of our five senses. Perhaps this is
why Paul encouraged us to be a "pleasing aroma of Christ."
We are to have such an impact on others that when they are
around us, thoughts and memories of Christ come to the forefront
of their minds without our saying even one word.

Emily

Shine like a star

*Let your light shine before men in such a way that they may
see your good works, and glorify your Father who is in heaven.*
Matthew 5:16 NASB

You have been called and divinely enabled to glow like a star,
in a sense, for God. You have been created to glorify your
Creator. Glorifying God is what separates the Christian from the
Christlike. God has given you a stage—your everyday life—so
that you can perform before an audience He has hand-picked for
you—your family, friends, co-workers and everyone whose life
intersects yours—in order to make Himself known in a way that
brings Him glory.

One day we will all stand upon the most important stage of all, but
we will not perform or compete. Instead we will face an audience
of One, and that One will judge us according to the performance
we gave during our time on earth. All that will matter then is
whether our brief, earthly life glorified Him in an eternal and
everlasting way. So, from this day on, commit to giving God the
performance of a lifetime by glorifying Him in your ordinary,
everyday life.

Laurie

The immoral woman

*For the lips of an immoral woman are as sweet as honey,
and her mouth is smoother than oil. But in the end she is
as bitter as poison, as dangerous as a double-edged sword.
Her feet go down to death; her steps lead straight to the grave.
For she cares nothing about the path to life. She staggers
down a crooked trail and doesn't realize it.*
Proverbs 5:3-6 NLT

The Immoral Woman has become so mainstream and so popular that some people don't even recognize her for the heartbreaking, trouble-making, home-wrecking seductress that she is. As Christians, we must not underestimate the peril the Immoral Woman poses to us and to our families. This gal is dangerous. Thankfully, God's Word enables us to identify her so that we can train our sons and daughters to avoid her and warn our husbands as well. But there is another reason we need to take a long, hard scriptural look at the Immoral Woman: we must make sure that our lives bear absolutely no resemblance whatsoever to hers.

Laurie

Carry it to completion

He who began a good work in you will carry it on
to completion until the day of Christ Jesus.
Philippians 1:6 NIV

You may have times when you feel as if God's ways are impossible to find, much less to follow. You feel as if you've been given a pieced-together pirate's map with cryptic symbols, no legend, and a tiny illusive X that marks the spot of some buried treasure that you're not sure is even worth finding. Is there any hope in completing the journey? You're really not sure.

Rest assured. He will not abandon you halfway through your process of redemption. He won't just point you in the general direction of His plan for your life and sit back laughing each time you veer off course. No. He created you; He wants to finish you. He began transforming your heart and your mind; He wants to complete the transformation. He laid out the path to total reconciliation with Him through Christ, and He wants to carry you the whole way there.

Emily

Attitude plus action

Fear of the Lord is the foundation of wisdom.
Knowledge of the Holy One results in good judgment.
Proverbs 9:10 NLT

The fear of the Lord is a very positive and beneficial thing. It is where true wisdom begins. So what exactly is it?

Very simply, the fear of the Lord is reverence for God that results in obedience to God. It is both attitude (reverence) and action (obedience); and when you put them together, you get wisdom! Before you begin your day, submit yourself in reverence before God in prayer, and commit to obey Him. Then watch for wisdom to show up.

Laurie

Zealous, not jealous

A heart at peace gives life to the body, but envy rots the bones.
Proverbs 14:30 NIV

The Bible is clear that jealousy is a serious no-no. In fact, it's so serious that it's in the same list as other headline-making sins like witchcraft and immorality (Gal. 5:19-21)! Yikes!

So what do we do with the green-eyed monster that lives inside each of us? Sometimes, the most effective weapon is also the most difficult to use. It is completely contradictory to everything you want to do, but when you do it, it has miraculous results: Don't get jealous, get zealous!

What does that mean? It means that you become zealous— enthusiastic, passionate, and excited – about how God has blessed that person, so much so that you begin praying that God would bless her even more!

If you become bitter that a friend gets to go on a fabulous trip to Italy, pray that her trip would be the experience of her lifetime! If someone excels in her career at a lightning speed and you find yourself jealous that yours isn't moving as quickly, pray that God would bless her even more!

At first it might feel unnatural to pray for God's blessings through the bitterness, but when you do, your heart begins to change. As you see God continue to bless that person, instead of taking that as an injustice against you, you see it as an answer to your own prayers! Their blessings become your blessings and your envy is free to turn into thanksgiving!

Emily

Can God?

Jesus looked at them intently and said, "Humanly speaking,
it is impossible. But with God everything is possible."
Matthew 19:26 NLT

*O*mnipotent is a word used to describe God and it simply means *all powerful*. But if you've ever thought about, wondered about or struggled with the question of God's power, words like *omnipotent* don't necessarily have the emotional weight you might be looking for. Chances are, you question God's power because you want to know if God can do something specific.

- Can God heal my marriage/my child/my cancer/my mind?
- Can God bring peace overseas/with my in-laws/at work/to my spirit?
- Can God control the rain/the hurricane/the tornadoes/the drought?
- Can God provide financial help/power over my addiction/a job for my husband?
- Can God save me/my son/my sister/our nation?

When considering God's power, most people don't care if He can control the universe, they just want to know if He can control *their* universe.

Can God? The answer is, "Yes He can."

Emily

The next generation

*We will not hide these truths from our children; we will tell
the next generation about the glorious deeds of the Lord,
about his power and his mighty wonders.*
Psalm 78:4 NLT

God wants you to share what He's done in your life with
others. As you share—as you brag on God—you're giving
Him glory. Whether or not you have children, God is still calling
you to share His glory with the next generation so their faith will
be strengthened and encouraged.

Today, ask God to show you someone who needs to hear about
the glorious deeds He has done in your life, then tell them.

Laurie

Rich with righteousness

God made him who had no sin to be sin for us,
so that in him we might become the righteousness of God.
2 Corinthians 5:21 NIV

There is more to your salvation than the forgiveness of your sins. Christ died to forgive you, yes. Because of His blood, your sins can be forgiven and you can be washed clean. But it doesn't stop there.

When God erases our sins, He does not leave us as a morally neutral blank slate. Instead, He takes that blank slate and pours upon it the righteousness of Christ. So we are not just bankrupt of sin; we are rich with righteousness—the righteousness of Christ.

Emily

Be careful

*But you must be careful so that your freedom does not
cause others with a weaker conscience to stumble.*
I Corinthians 8:9 NLT

When you're around your children, your teenagers or even people in your church or Bible study group who are new believers, you must be very careful. You, being more mature in your faith and having a greater knowledge of your freedom in Christ, understand that God's grace trumps legalism. Your younger brothers and sisters in Christ, however, may still be working through their own lists of dos and don'ts. Watch yourself closely so that your liberties in the gray areas of life do not cause someone who still sees things as black and white to stumble.

Laurie

Salt of the earth

*You are the salt of the earth. But if the salt loses its saltiness,
how can it be made salty again? It is no longer good for anything,
except to be thrown out and trampled underfoot.*
Matthew 5:13 NIV

Salt is used for many things, and as the salt of the earth, we can learn a lot from the way salt is used. First, salt preserves things. Just as it slows down and prevents decay in food, we should do all that we can to prevent spiritual decay in others. Secondly, just as salt adds flavor to food, we should add "flavor" to others by enhancing their lives and being a blessing to them.

Lastly, salt creates thirst. When others spend time with you, do they leave thirsty for more of God because they can see how satisfied you are with Him? Do they want more of what they see in you?

Emily

August

Mat carriers

Four men arrived carrying a paralyzed man on a mat.
They couldn't bring him to Jesus because of the crowd,
so they dug a hole through the roof above his head.
Then they lowered the man on his mat, right
down in front of Jesus. Seeing their faith,
Jesus said to the paralyzed man,
"My child, your sins are forgiven."
Mark 2:3-5 NLT

It is so easy to be a great friend in theory. You can make empty promises, pledge undying devotion and promise to be BFFs 'til the day you die. But what happens when your friend has a flat tire, or a sick child or a deployed husband? What happens when her need becomes an inconvenience? Do you still help her? Or do you point to the fine print of your friendship and stand on a foundation of every woman for herself?

These four men were determined to help their paralyzed friend even though it wasn't convenient. When a simple solution wouldn't work, they found another way, determined to put their friendship into action. Ultimately these mat carriers did for their friend what he could not do for himself: they brought him closer to Jesus.

Emily

Change your posture

[Hannah] said, "May your servant find favor in your eyes."
Then she went her way and ate something,
and her face was no longer downcast.
I Samuel 1:18 NIV

When Hannah cried out to the Lord because she longed for a child, her grief had an element of whine to it—so much so that the prophet Eli thought she was drunk! But after she poured her heart out to God, Hannah changed her posture. She got up, "went her way and ate something, and her face was no longer downcast."

When you're tempted to whine, it helps to change something about yourself physically. Get up. Take a shower. Get dressed. Eat. Exercise. Put on makeup. Fix your hair. Brush your teeth.

For a face that is no longer downcast, pour your heart out to God and then follow up with a little change in your posture just like Hannah did.

Emily

3C syndrome

It is better to live alone in the desert
than with a crabby complaining wife.
Proverbs 21:19 NLT

We've all met this woman before haven't we? But let's be honest: at times, we've all been this woman, too. And while these verses may specifically apply to married women, you and I both know that crabbiness does not discriminate. Anyone (married or single, young or old, male or female, Christian or non-Christian) can exhibit the classic symptoms of what I call "3C Syndrome": (1) Contentiousness, (2) Crabbiness, with frequent bouts of (3) Complaining. Fortunately, 3C is not generally contagious, and there is a cure.

We'll look at the cure a little closer tomorrow, but for now, know that it begins with Proverbs 16:24: "Kind words are like honey—Sweet to the soul and healthy for the body" (NLT).

Laurie

3 B speech

*Let no unwholesome word proceed from your mouth,
but only such a word as is good for edification according to
the need of the moment, so that it will give grace to those who hear.*
Ephesians 4:29 NASB

Ephesians 4:29 gives us three divine boundaries for every word we speak. First, we must choose words that are "good" (*agathos* in the Greek), which is defined as "benevolent and beneficial."[8] Second, our words must edify (*oikodome* in the Greek), which means to "build up and spiritually profit" others.[9] The final criteria for the words we choose is that they must "give grace" (*charis* in the Greek) which means to bless and benefit others.[10]

What does all of this mean to us? Very simply, it means that the words that flow from our lips must do three things: build, bless and benefit. This is 3B speech—the cure for 3C syndrome that we looked at yesterday. Furthermore, we're to speak these words in a way that illustrates and emulates God's grace, which means even if the hearer has not earned and does not deserve to hear 3B words, we must speak them anyway.

Do these boundaries mean we cannot correct, discipline or honestly express ourselves to others? Absolutely not. But it does mean we must do it in a positive, gracious way with the motivation of building up, not tearing down.

Laurie

August 5

Eternal work

*Do not work for food that spoils, but for food that
endures to eternal life, which the Son of Man will give you.
For on him God the Father has placed his seal of approval.*
John 6:27 NIV

You don't have to work at a church or a ministry to maintain
an eternal perspective. Any time you work with people, there
is opportunity for God to do something eternally significant.
Many times, it's not the job itself that is difficult; it's the people
you work with. But when you start seeing your demanding boss
as someone who needs Jesus or your frustrating customers as
people who need to experience the love of God, it makes it easier
to find significance in your job. God might have you in the midst of
the vocational lion's den simply so that, through you, others may
see Him.

Emily

Rejoice always

The Lord will command His lovingkindness in the daytime;
and His song will be with me in the night.
Psalm 42:8 NASB

It is natural and even easy to sing, praise, and rejoice in the Lord during the sunny, daytime, blue-sky seasons of life. But it is supernatural and even miraculous to sing and rejoice during the cold, dark seasons of the night. However, God has given us a song—a reason to rejoice—every day, every night, in every season of our lives.

First Thessalonians 5:16 says, "Rejoice always" (NASB). Other versions say "Rejoice evermore" (KJV), "Always be joyful" (NLT), and "Be cheerful no matter what" (MSG).

Are you singing a fair-weather song? Is your joy dependent on the time of day? Is your ability to rejoice conditional? Your song will remain as long as you're singing His song. He is the Song Giver, and when you sing His song, all who witness your life will see the evidence of His lovingkindness.

Laurie

Is it guilt or conviction?

Who will bring any charge against those whom God has chosen?
It is God who justifies. Who then is the one who condemns?
No one. Christ Jesus who died—more than that, who was raised
to life—is at the right hand of God and is also interceding for us.
Romans 8:33-34 NIV

Guilt and conviction can both feel like a weight on your shoulders, a punch in your gut or a whisper in your ear that never seems to go away. The right way to deal with guilt is to fight it with the truth. Conquer the feelings until they at last surrender to the truth. But the right way to deal with conviction is to embrace it. Change and grow and repent until at last *you* have surrendered to the truth.

Such similar beginnings yet such different responses. And the consequences for misinterpreting one for the other are a neutral life, a life of regret or a life of second-best.

To avoid misinterpreting guilt and conviction, you must learn their differences. They are slight, but significant. Take the time to prayerfully consider your feelings and you will be better able to categorize them accurately as Guilt or Conviction.

- Guilt is from Satan; conviction is from the Holy Spirit.
- Guilt causes paralysis; conviction causes growth.
- Guilt points to problems; conviction points to solutions.
- Guilt builds doubt; conviction builds faith.
- Guilt leads to estrangement; conviction leads to relationship.

Emily

Stumbling block

We put no stumbling block in anyone's path,
so that our ministry will not be discredited.
2 Corinthians 6:3 NIV

Sin affects your intimacy with God. Your intimacy with God affects your ability to reflect His glory. And your ability to reflect His glory affects your ministry, or your witness.

Paul constantly encouraged his fellow believers to overcome the sins they were struggling with because he knew that they could become stumbling blocks to others. Their sins were preventing them from glorifying God through their individual lives and through their churches. In order to spread the gospel, they first needed to address the sins in their own lives.

What sin are you struggling with? Since it's preventing you from glorifying God, it's also becoming a stumbling block to those around you.

Laurie

Serve with humility

*As for me, may I never boast about anything
except the cross of our Lord Jesus Christ.*
Galatians 6:14 NLT

There was once a man who displayed a beautiful prize-winning orchid as the centerpiece on his dining room table. All throughout dinner, his guests talked about the flower's beauty. When dinner was over and they retreated to the sitting room, the host asked his guests if anyone could remember what the vase looked like that held the orchid. No one could.

When you serve the Lord with humility, people will see Him instead of you, His vessel. Everything we do is nothing if others end up seeing us and our accomplishments rather than the cross of Christ. Serve with humility in a way that brings attention to God and not yourself. Remain forever in His shadow.

Emily

Prudence

> Listen as Wisdom calls out!
> Hear as understanding raises her voice!..
> By the gates at the entrance to the town,
> on the road leading in, she cries aloud,
> "I call to you, to all of you! I raise my voice to all people.
> You simple people, use good judgment.
> You foolish people, show some understanding."
> Proverbs 8:1, 3-5 NLT

"Discretion" used to be one of those innocuous, vanilla-sounding words that I associated with, well, "boring." I knew it was closely related to the word "prudent" (another unpopular, seldom-used word) but to be honest, both words were a little yawn-inducing to me. Not anymore.

God's Word has completely changed the negative connotations I used to associate with the words "discretion" and "prudence." Although I don't often use those specific words (and I'm guessing you probably don't either), I do use positive terms like "smart," "discerning," "spiritually sharp," and "wise" to describe discreet, prudent people. Whatever you may choose to call them, discretion and prudence are keys that can unlock your God-given potential.

Laurie

It all belongs to God

"Naked I came from my mother's womb, and naked I will depart.
The Lord gave and the Lord has taken away;
may the name of the Lord be praised."
Job 1:21 NIV

No one is immune to the struggle with money, materialism, greed and desire. It affects us all, and we all need to remind ourselves of the bigger picture. It all belongs to God.

Job's prayer is just as practical for a tornado victim as it is for a mom who is grocery shopping. It can apply to those living in penthouses and those living in someone's guest bedroom. It is useful for the 12-year-old boy mowing yards during the summer as well as the 75-year-old widow living off her husband's pension.

Everything belongs to the Lord. And although you are accountable for how you manage His stuff, He is not accountable to you. He gives and takes away at His own discretion. Blessed be His name.

Emily

My hope

May those who fear You rejoice when they see me,
for I have put my hope in Your word.
Psalm 119:74 NIV

Does seeing you or being with you bring joy to the hearts of others? When you are actively trusting and hoping in the Word of God, your life will cause other believers to rejoice, especially as they see you hoping and trusting in God in the midst of a difficult season. Lift up today's Psalm in prayer to God, and proclaim that you are not placing your hope in yourself, in your own strength, in another person, or in your current circumstances—no matter how good or bad they may be. Tell the Lord that you are placing your hope solely and completely in Him. Ask Him to allow you to reflect the hope you have in Him to others.

Laurie

The water paradox

Jesus answered her, "If you knew the gift of God and who it is that asks you for a drink, you would have asked him and he would have given you living water."
John 4:10 NIV

If you've ever encountered a hurricane, you know how destructive the storm's waters can be. However, in the aftermath of the storm, water is the first thing that people need. It has the power to renew, refresh, and completely cleanse like nothing else could. Water, which has the power to destroy, also has the power to save. It seems a paradox.

So, too, do God's justice and God's mercy seem to be a paradox. God's power is immeasurable. He alone holds infinite potential, infinite strength and infinite might, and it is for those reasons we should fear and respect Him. But along with His infinite power comes His infinite grace, for He alone has the ability to cleanse us. We are dirty, filthy, and caked with sin, and we need Him to cleanse us as only He can.

When Christ offered the woman at the well "living water," He was offering her a way to be forgiven and washed as white as snow. He offers us the same thing. We can choose to accept the living water and the saving power it brings, or we can choose to reject it and face the Lord's destructive power instead.

Emily

How glorious

Ascribe to the Lord the glory due His name;
bring an offering, and come into His courts.
Psalm 96:8 NIV

One of the biggest obstacles we face as we seek to glorify God is that we have forgotten just how glorious He is. Most of our waking hours are full to the brim with the routine responsibilities and activities of our daily lives. In our haste and hurry, we're often too busy and self-consumed to see the glory of God. We walk right past it every day, but we don't see it. And because we don't see it, we've forgotten the glory of the One we consistently and routinely refer to as "God." Yet every day without fail, our faithful, invisible God visibly makes His glory known.

Today, take a mental journey far away from your busy life and crazy calendar. Escape for a few minutes from your current roles, routines, and responsibilities. Gain a fresh glimpse of God's glory and allow Him to show you His splendor and majesty in a brand new way.

Laurie

Ego

Pride goes before destruction, and haughtiness before a fall.
Proverbs 16:18 NLT

There are some big egos in the Bible. King Nebuchadnezzar who made a huge gold statue of himself and demanded that all bow down and worship him. King Darius who declared that everyone must pray to him alone for thirty days. King Herod who ordered that all male children under two be slaughtered because he was afraid of the newborn King of the Jews.

I've often wondered what the point of such power is if what comes with it is a constant state of paranoia that someone will come and take that power away from you. However, I see the same egotistical tendencies appear again and again, not just across the generations, but even in my own life. Pride. Ego. Paranoia. Controlling tendencies. All of it surfacing from a fear that letting go will mean that you don't get what you want.

But the truth is, by letting go and humbling yourself to God, you get what you really need.

Emily

High and low

The Lord gave and the Lord has taken away;
may the name of the Lord be praised.
Job 1:21 NIV

Isn't it amazing how quickly your day can go from good to bad? Sure, you may have some prolonged periods of ease with very few problems and relatively little strife, but that's not the norm. Most of your days are a combination of both good and bad, high and low.

Learning how to handle the highs and lows of everyday life is a significant step towards living a life that glorifies God. Praise Him in the good days *and* in the not-so-good days. Glorify Him from the mountain top *as well as* the valley. Like Job, lift up His name when He gives *and* when He takes away.

Laurie

Close only counts

*When Jesus heard his answer, he said, "There is still
one thing you haven't done. Sell all your possessions and
give the money to the poor, and you will have treasure in heaven.
Then come, follow me." But when the man heard this
he became very sad, for he was very rich.*

Luke 18:22-23 NLT

Unfortunately, it's not uncommon to be so close to Christ and still miss out on Him and His best for our lives. The Bible is full of people who were so close. Consider the rich, young ruler. He asked the right question to the right person and received the right answer. The problem was that he couldn't imagine that his life could be better than it was right then. He was so close to a having an amazing (eternal) life, but chose his really good (temporary) life instead.

In Christianity, it's our actions that matter, not our intentions, so being close doesn't count. Do you have good intentions? Are you close to obeying God? Consider how you can transform those intentions into actions and pray for clarity to know the difference.

I've often heard it said that "Close only counts in horseshoes and hand grenades." While I don't know if that's true or not, I do know that I don't want to stand before our Lord one day and hear Him say, "My child, you were so close…"

Emily

Trust Him now

Then call on me when you are in trouble,
and I will rescue you, and you will give me glory.
Psalm 50:15 NLT

Glorifying God in the future often begins by calling on Him and trusting Him today.

Are you trusting the Lord in whatever trials and struggles you're facing right now? If so, by faith claim the promise contained within today's Psalm, and prayerfully commit to glorify Him, even as you wait for Him to rescue you.

Laurie

Power in the ordinary

*The Son radiates God's own glory and expresses
the very character of God, and he sustains everything
by the mighty power of his command.*
Hebrews 1:3 NLT

God's power is not just reserved for major trials, questions or needs. It's also evident in the small, everyday things that we're so accustomed to that we brush them off as ordinary.

The truth is, there is nothing ordinary about the fact that you have breath. That the sun remains in its place. That rain falls. That your body can digest food, fight an infection, or grow a baby while you sleep.

The thing that looks ordinary and simple and, dare I say, unimpressive, is actually God's great power at work.

Emily

Beautiful submission

For wives, this means submit to your husbands as to the Lord.
For a husband is the head of his wife as Christ is the head
of the church. He is the Savior of his body, the church.
As the church submits to Christ, so you wives should
submit to your husbands in everything.
Ephesians 5:22-24 NLT

The Bible clearly teaches that women are to submit to their own husbands (not to every man, but to their own husbands), and that husbands are to love their wives as Christ loved the church. Submission basically means that women are to respectfully place themselves under the authority of their husbands.

The scriptural principles of submission do not imply that women are inferior to men. On the contrary, Scripture emphasizes the equality of men and women: "God created man in His own image, in the image of God He created him; male and female He created them" (Gen. 1:27 NASB). But even before the fall of man, Adam and Eve had different roles. From the beginning, God created man to lead the home and woman to be his helper (Gen. 2:18). And until the fall, Eve's submission to Adam wasn't a problem; but after the fall, it became a major problem.

Now just in case you're upset (or a little offended) by the concept of submission, please take time to read Philippians 2:5–11. This beautiful passage reveals that Christ, who is equal with God, willingly submitted Himself to God when He came to this earth and died on the cross to save us. In this way, Christ is an example to all of us (men and women alike) of the beauty and importance of submission.

Laurie

Hide or seek

*"Can anyone hide in secret places
so that I cannot see him?" declares the Lord.*
Jeremiah 23:24 NIV

There are many times when we, in our Christian walks, cover our eyes in an effort to hide from God. Perhaps we are ashamed of our sin, so we quit looking at Him, and somehow believe that because we cannot see God, He cannot see us either. But He can.

Maybe we quit going to church because we think we won't run into God anywhere else. We quit reading our Bibles because we think that will silence Him. We bury ourselves under a tunnel of apathy, and stay there so long that we come to believe that God has forgotten about us because He can no longer see us. But the reality is that it is we who can no longer see Him anymore, not the other way around.

Do not try to hide from God because you will never be hidden. Do not try to forget about God because He will never forget you. With God, there is no choice to hide or seek. There is only seek.

Emily

Grace upon grace

Let us then approach God's throne of grace with confidence,
so that we may receive mercy and find grace
to help us in our time of need.
Hebrews 4:16 NIV

No matter where you are or what you've done, God wants to give you grace. He can give you a second and a third and a fourth chance. In fact, no matter how many times you have fallen, you can still receive the grace of God. "Out of his fullness we have all received grace in place of grace already given" (John 1:16 NIV).

But beware because your messy past is going to try to make a comeback. Where God's plan is grace, Satan has a counterfeit plan. His plan is to bring up your past and get you to stumble into your old messes over and over again. He is going to try to pull you back and maybe pull you further under than you were before.

God's grace is imperative if you want to keep your messy past in the past.

Laurie

Forgiven

Jesus straightened up and asked her, "Woman, where are they?
Has no one condemned you?" "No one, sir," she said.
"Then neither do I condemn you," Jesus declared.
"Go now and leave your life of sin."
John 8:10-11 NIV

Imagine that Jesus is having dinner. The restaurant is fancy. The table is exquisite. The menu, mouthwatering. And that's how you see it when your worst enemy drags you into the fancy restaurant after catching you in the middle of the worst sin you've ever committed.

Maybe you're drunk. Maybe you're high. Maybe your hands are full of things you've stolen. Maybe you're only half dressed. Whatever the situation, you clearly do not belong. They parade you in like a dessert tray, and make you stop in front of Jesus. You're embarrassed. You want to run away. You wish you could crawl under a rock. But instead, Jesus stands up, pulls the chair out for you, and motions for you to sit down.

Clearly, you've been forgiven.

Emily

I urge Euodia and I urge Syntyche to live in harmony in the Lord.
Philippians 4:2 NASB

Have you ever been around two women who could not get along because of a petty disagreement? It happens all the time, even in church, and it happened in Paul's days to these two women in the church of Philippi. But Paul urges them to put aside their differences and live in harmony.

I love the word *harmony*. Harmony means we're all singing the same song, but we're singing it in four different parts. It's the perfect analogy for how we should behave as Christians. Personalities, spiritual gifts or even callings may vary from person to person, but we're still to live in harmony by all singing the same music—the music of the Gospel of Jesus Christ. We can proclaim it differently as long as we proclaim it faithfully together.

Laurie

All things

And we know that in all things God works for the good of those who love him, who have been called according to his purpose.
Romans 8:28 NIV

God is in control and is able to work all things for good. This doesn't mean that all things *are* good. Not at all. It just means that God can take all things and work them *into* something good.

Imagine eating a whole cup of flour by itself, chomping on a stick of butter, washing it down with a few raw eggs, and polishing it off with a handful of raw sugar. Separately, those ingredients would be disgusting. But when you add some baking powder, stir it all together, and submit it to extreme heat, you get something delicious after time—cake!

God's power is always at work behind the scenes, taking all of the bad things, filtering them through His knowledge, His holiness, and His love, in order to make something beautiful come of it. This is His sovereignty at work.

Emily

Heavenly minded

Set your minds on things above, not on earthly things.
Colossians 3:2 NIV

In these temporary, earthbound bodies, we're very prone to temporary, earthbound thinking—and living. We get stuck in the grind and routine of the present. We get trapped in the thoughts and cares of today. We get caught up and consumed with the temporal. We forget that there's more to life than what we can see here on earth. Much more.

Instead, we are commanded to be heavenly-minded. To resist the gravitational pull of our earthbound mindset. Today, change your focus from the temporal reality of the things that are seen to the eternal reality of the unseen—your eternal home and the glory to come. Your future is bright and on that day, you really are gonna *glo*, girl!

Laurie

Take a stand

*Therefore put on the full armor of God, so that when
the day of evil comes, you may be able to stand your ground,
and after you have done everything, to stand.*
Ephesians 6:13 NASB

Many people read about the armor of God and assume that we are supposed to wear it so that we will be prepared to fight. However, Paul tells us to put on the armor not so we can fight, but so we can *stand*. I think of the guards at Buckingham Palace or the secret service agents that protect the President. They are trained to stand guard, to be alert, ready, and free from distraction. Their very presence is meant to deter any attacks before they even happen.

The armor of God is important because the ultimate defense is the ability to make your enemy run before there is even a fight! "Submit yourselves, then, to God. Resist the devil, and he will flee from you" (Jas. 4:7 NIV).

Emily

Meditate on His works

They speak of the glorious splendor of your majesty—
and I will meditate on your wonderful works.
Psalm 145:5 NIV

Meditation is a command. It is listed over twenty times in the Bible, and alluded to many more times than that. In fact, it is the very key to getting God's Word from your head to your heart. It is thinking about the Bible in a very intentional way.

Many people have said that if you know how to worry, you know how to meditate. Worry is simply allowing your mind to wander and "what-ifing" about every negative outcome you could possibly have. Meditation is simply taking that same God-given gift of imagination and applying it to God's Word. It is thinking deliberate thoughts about a deliberate God.

Emily

Ignore criticism

As King David came to Bahurim,
a man came out of the village cursing them.
2 Samuel 16:5 NLT

Even the best leaders will have their critics. David definitely had his. One was a man named Shimei who publicly criticized and cursed David and even threw stones at him and his men. One of the men requested permission to retaliate and kill Shimei, but David said no. "Leave him alone and let him curse... And perhaps the Lord will see that I am being wronged and will bless me because of these curses today" (2 Sam. 16:11-12 NLT).

David knew that his job was to respond to the Lord, not to respond to criticism. And because he knew that he was in the Lord's will, he was not distracted by the threats and harsh words of others. Your leadership depends upon your refusing to lash out at those who criticize you. They may throw stones, but instead of throwing them back, use them to build an altar.

Laurie

Full of grace

*They sharpen their tongues like swords
and aim cruel words like deadly arrows.*
Psalm 64:3 NIV

No matter how much you bite your tongue, there will still be times when your words come out like weapons of destruction. The Bible likens our words to sharpened swords, deadly arrows and even poisonous venom (Ps. 140:3). In your own power, you are not strong enough to tame your tongue. Left to your own devices, your words will continue to wound, kill and destroy.

Thankfully, there is something stronger than your words. Grace. "Let your conversation be always full of grace," (Col. 4:6 NIV). When you immerse yourself in the grace of the Lord, your heart becomes filled with His grace. And when your heart is full of grace, your words will follow.

Emily

August 31

Selfishness

For I can testify that they gave not only what they
could afford, but far more.
2 Corinthians 8:3 NLT

When your neighbor gets new carpet, does your own carpet suddenly look shabbier? When a friend gets a new car, does your own car suddenly seem old, ugly and outdated? If you feel deprived when others are blessed, you may be suffering from that childish ailment called selfishness.

Selfishness is the constant need to covet what others have. It makes it difficult, if not impossible, to rejoice with others when the Lord blesses their lives and it prevents you from glorifying God. The opposite of selfishness is Christlike sacrificial giving. So when you find yourself constantly saying, "I want," combat the selfishness by becoming a giver instead of a taker.

Laurie

september

September 1

Risk of rejection

When one of the Pharisees invited Jesus to have dinner with him,
he went to the Pharisee's house and reclined at the table.
A woman in that town who lived a sinful life learned that
Jesus was eating at the Pharisee's house, so she
came there with an alabaster jar of perfume.
Luke 7:36-37 NIV

When we hear the story of the woman who broke the alabaster jar of perfume at the foot of Jesus, we often focus on what a humble act of surrender her brave gesture was. What a commendable risk she took when she shattered such a valuable asset.

But we often overlook that this woman took an even greater risk before she ever sat at Jesus' feet. Notice who was at the table with Jesus. All men. Pharisees. Yet despite the social implications of her actions, this woman came, uninvited, and interrupted the meal of men. She knew that she could have easily been turned away, if not by Jesus then by the other men. But she was willing to risk rejection in order to bless Jesus.

Emily

Risk of embarrassment

As she stood behind him at his feet weeping,
she began to wet his feet with her tears.
Then she wiped them with her hair,
kissed them and poured perfume on them.
Luke 7:38 NIV

This woman's gesture of anointing Jesus' head and feet was very unconventional. Typically, a woman's family would purchase an alabaster box and fill it with ointment when she came of marrying age so that, when a man asked for her hand, she could respond by breaking it at his feet and anointing him with her perfume.

When this woman took this tradition out of its original intended context of marriage, she risked being humiliated. She risked someone saying, "You fool! You're not supposed to do it that way. You're supposed to hold on to your alabaster box and save it for your bridegroom! Don't you know the custom at all?" But she wasn't afraid of the humiliation because Jesus was more important to her than her pride. She was willing to risk embarrassment in order to bless Jesus.

Emily

Risk of failure

While he was in Bethany, reclining at the table in the home
of Simon the Leper, a woman came with an alabaster jar of
very expensive perfume, made of pure nard. She broke
the jar and poured the perfume on his head.
Mark 14:3 NIV

There is a telling word in the story of the woman with the alabaster jar - the word *broke*. Alabaster boxes were made in such a way that the only way for someone to get the perfume out would be to break the entire container it was in. There was no "a little squirt here" or "a little there." It was all or nothing. And for this woman, it was all. She *broke* the jar. She didn't crack it. She didn't poke a hole in it. She broke it in such a way that it could never be unbroken.

If this rash, risky act on the woman's part somehow backfired, she would have no second chance. She could not try again. But, she was willing to risk complete failure in order to bless Jesus.

Emily

Take the risk

You did not give me a kiss, but this woman, from the
time I entered, has not stopped kissing my feet.
You did not put oil on my head, but she
has poured perfume on my feet.
Luke 7:45 NIV

Most of you have probably come to a point where you've decided to trust Jesus as your savior. You've even made Him Lord of your life and are trying your best to live for Him. But have you taken that next step where you've brought *everything*—the *entire* contents of your alabaster box—and poured it at His feet with reckless abandonment?

Have you taken the risk? Have you gone out of your way to say, "Yes. Whatever you want, whenever you want, I want to be a blessing! I want to pour out my time to bless you. I want to pour out my money to bless you. I want to pour out my talents and my gifts to bless you. I want to pour our every last drop to serve you better!"?

Emily

Being judgmental

Do not judge, or you too will be judged.
Matthew 7:1 NIV

In the world, Christians are often accused of being judgmental and intolerant. Some may even quote Matthew 7:1 to us when we challenge their ways with God's truth. In order to approach judgment with a righteous attitude and not a self-righteous one, consider these seven guidelines:

1. Do not make rash, unjust or unkind judgments.

2. Do make judgments based upon wisdom and discernment.

3. Before making any judgment, you must first judge yourself and ask the Lord to examine your heart and reveal any hidden sin.

4. You must only judge what you can see—outward actions. Do not attribute motives to another person because only the Lord can see the heart.

5. You must address and judge sin within the church.

6. Where there is not direct biblical prohibition concerning a matter, we are not to judge other Christians.

7. When the world opposes God and His Word, stand with God and uphold His Word.

Laurie

Helpful words

The lips of the godly speak helpful words.
Proverbs 10:32 NLT

When you listen to the internal monologue going on in your mind, do your words spark thanksgiving, or do they spark complaining? The difference can be as subtle as using "get to" instead of "have to." For example, when you say you "have to" clean your house, you're implying that the task is an unwelcome chore and you're merely a slave to the mess. When you say you "get to" clean your house, you're subtly reminding yourself that you're blessed enough to have a home, you're blessed with material possessions to fill the home and you're blessed with the physical ability to clean the home. "Have to" is the beginning of whining. "Get to" is the beginning of thanksgiving.

Choosing the right words can lead to a transformation of your attitude. So use helpful words, even when you're just talking to yourself.

Emily

September 7

The throne room

So let us come boldly to the throne of our gracious God.
There we will receive his mercy, and we will find grace
to help us when we need it most.
Hebrews 4:16 NLT

Are you hesitant to come to the throne room of the Lord? His Word says that you can come *boldly*. Not meekly, not barely, not occasionally, but *boldly* because you *belong*.

Once there, you won't be met by a judgmental, I'm-so-mad-at-you, you've-messed-up-so-badly, what-are-you-doing-here-in-my-throne-room type of God. Oh, no. You'll be met by a gracious God. And although you may expect to receive rebuke, discipline or condemnation, the Bible says that you will instead receive mercy, grace and help.

Will you run to His throne room today?

Laurie

God's masterpiece

For we are God's masterpiece.
Ephesians 2:10 NLT

This word *masterpiece* is especially significant in this verse and deserves a closer look. The Greek transliteration of this word is "poiema," and it means "a work of art or a masterpiece."[11] But if you look at this Greek word closely, you'll see that there's an English word contained within it. It's the word "poem." Isn't that beautiful! And when you put all of this information together, this verse is actually saying: "For we are God's poem, God's masterpiece, God's work of art."

Have you forgotten that you are a work of art to God? You are His labor of love, the fruit of His creativity, an expression of His image.

Laurie

Joy in work

*The Lord God took the man and put him in the
Garden of Eden to work it and take care of it.*
Genesis 2:15 NIV

Many people incorrectly assume that work is a punishment—a result of the fall of man. But the truth is, God commanded man to work before sin entered the world. Work is a privilege. It's a way to partner with God, to fulfill your purpose, and to make the best use out of one of God's creations (you!) Even if you don't find joy in your job, you can still find joy in your work.

Emily

His book

Consider how I love Your precepts; Revive me, O Lord,
according to Your lovingkindness.
Psalm 119:159 NKJV

If you read a book over and over again, it always turns out just like it did the first time you read it. But when you read the Word of God, it is new and fresh no matter how often you read it. Its message is deeper and its words are richer every time you open its pages. No other book captivates, stimulates, and motivates like God's Word does. If you want to fall deeper in love with the Lord, fall in love with His book.

Emily

September 11

Reputation of love

A new command I give you: Love one another.
As I have loved you, so you must love one another.
By this everyone will know that you are my disciples,
if you love one another.
John 13:34-35 NIV

Before Jesus went to the cross, He knew He was leaving behind a legacy for His disciples. He knew that people would form an opinion of them based on the simple fact that they followed Him. And because of that, He gave them the promise of a good reputation.

What was Jesus' reputation? It was a reputation of love. Everything He did, He did out of love. When He cleared the temple, He did so out of love. When He healed the sick, He did so out of love. When He challenged the rich young ruler, He did so out of love. When He confronted the woman caught in adultery, He did so out of love.

And finally, when He went to the cross, He did so out of love.

Are you being being driven by love? Motivated by love? Inspired by love? God *is* love, and Jesus displayed the ultimate act of love when He died on the cross. Do you want to point others to Him? Build a reputation of love.

Emily

Possible

*Jesus looked at them intently and said,
"Humanly speaking, it is impossible,
but with God everything is possible."*
Matthew 19:26 NLT

What impossible dream is God calling you to believe today? What impossible person have you been praying for year after year after year? What impossible situation do you go to bed thinking about and face each morning?

Have you forgotten that *impossible* is what God does best?

- He enabled two 90-somethings, Abraham and Sarah, to have a son.

- He enabled Moses to part the Red Sea, save the Israelites and defeat the Egyptian army.

- He enabled the sound of Israel's trumpets to take down Jericho's wall.

- He enabled a single stone to defeat a giant.

- He enabled a virgin to bring forth a Son to save sinners like you and me.

Some days we're blessed to experience a long series of pinch-me moments. On those days, the words "exceedingly abundantly above all that we ask or think" (Eph. 3:20 NKJV) replay over and over in our heads like an endless loop. So if God did the impossible yesterday, why do we doubt that He'll do the impossible today?

Emily

September 13

Beginning with I

> *The acts of the flesh are obvious: sexual immorality,*
> *impurity and debauchery; idolatry and witchcraft; hatred,*
> *discord, jealousy, fits of rage, selfish ambition, dissensions, factions*
> *and envy; drunkenness, orgies, and the like. I warn you, as I did before,*
> *that those who live like this will not inherit the kingdom of God.*
> Galatians 5:19-21 NIV

The Bible says that the acts of the flesh (or acts of the sinful nature) are obvious. But sometimes, even though they can be very easy to recognize in the lives of others, they can be difficult to recognize in your own life.

The acts of the flesh fall into three categories, and each category has something in common. They all begin with "I."

- Immorality - sexual immorality, impurity and debauchery

- Idolatry - idolatry and witchcraft

- Intimacy with others - hatred, discord, jealousy, fits of rage, selfish ambition, dissensions, factions, envy

- Impulses - drunkenness, orgies

If it is difficult for you to notice the acts of the flesh in your own life, ask yourself one simple question: "Am I beginning with 'I' or am I beginning with 'He?'"

Emily

Examine our ways

> Let us examine our ways and test them,
> and let us return to the Lord.
> Lamentations 3:40 NIV

Sometimes, for many different reasons (busyness, weariness, guilt, shame, fear, anger or despair), we ignore God's command to examine our lives. We allow life's seasons to come and go without ever seeking to understand His purposes in them. As a result, our lives become shallow, a succession of seasons bereft of meaning and value. Those who follow God's instructions to examine their lives will gain understanding, insight and wisdom which will enable them to experience a life of purpose, meaning and eternal significance.

Will you allow God to examine your life? Will you earnestly seek to understand His purpose for each season? If you will, the wisdom you gain will allow you to grow in your walk with Him, to know Him in a more intimate way and, perhaps, to rediscover His glorious and meaningful plan for your life. Don't wait for the waves of a stormy season to force you "out to sea" in your walk with God. Open the eyes of your heart to what God has to show you.

Laurie

Vent to God

*If I had really spoken this way to others,
I would have been a traitor to your people...
Then I went into your sanctuary, O God, and
I finally understood the destiny of the wicked.*
Psalm 73:15, 17 NLT

One of the most beautiful and amazing things in this Psalm of Asaph is his honesty and openness before God. He did not vent his frustrations to everyone who crossed his path (as we are often prone to do). Instead, he held his tongue and saved his innermost thoughts for God, holding nothing back from Him.

God knows your thoughts even before you think them, which is all the more reason why you can safely bring them before Him. If you're hurting, disappointed, bitter, unhappy, depressed or even fuming mad, spend some extended time with the Lord in prayer. Resist the urge to vent to one of your friends, and pour it all out before God instead. Then, take a deep breath and turn your thoughts solely upon Him.

Laurie

Don't look back

*Brothers, listen! We are here to proclaim that
through this man Jesus there is forgiveness for your sins.*
Acts 13:38 NLT

I don't know about you, but I know that there are some things in my past that I'm not proud of. (And by "past" I mean my childhood, my teens, my young adult years and even my yesterday!) But here's what I know about the past: 1) Everyone has something in her past that she's not proud of, and 2) God can forgive it all!

Growing in Christ is not about looking backward and trying to undo those things that can't be undone. It's about accepting God's forgiveness and moving forward from where you are right now.

Emily

September 17

Mirror image

*Anyone who listens to the word but does not do what it says is
like someone who looks at his face in a mirror and, after looking
at himself, goes away and immediately forgets what he looks like.
But whoever looks intently into the perfect law that gives freedom,
and continues in it—not forgetting what they have heard,
but doing it—they will be blessed in what they do.*
James 1:23-25 NIV

God's Word is like a high-quality mirror. When you look intently at it, you will see God's standard and whether or not you are a reflection of that standard. Just like when you see yourself in a three-way mirror in a dressing room, you may be stunned by the reality of what you see as you look intently into the mirror of God's Word.

A literal mirror may or may not reveal your true physical flaws. In fact, some mirrors are "magic" mirrors. These are the ones we all love because they've been hung at a very slight angle that makes a very big difference. When you look into these kinds of mirrors you think, "Wow, I'm taller and slimmer than I thought I was!" But God's mirror—the Bible—is perfect. It will never lie to you. When you look at it, you will always see the truth about yourself—and you will be forced to make a decision.

You can choose to walk away and ignore the spiritually out-of-shape person you've become, or you'll choose to embrace the truth and allow God to shape you into His image.

Laurie

No cruise control

Never be lazy, but work hard and
serve the Lord enthusiastically.
Romans 12:11 NLT

It's easy to look in the mirror sometimes and see ourselves as worn out or "ruined." Maybe our bodies aren't what they used to be after years of having children. Maybe our homes are not as organized as we'd like because of the hours spent working or serving elsewhere. Maybe our hands are calloused or our skin is wrinkled from years of working in the sun.

But the truth is that work is a part of God's plan and His purpose for all of us, and when we don't work to the best of our abilities, we're sinning against Him. The Bible never tolerates the "cruise control" kind of lifestyle. Instead it commands a life of hard work, diligent service, and enthusiastic initiative.

Don't strive to get to the end of your life and still see yourself with a shiny new finish. Instead, strive to look back and see a life that is a little dull, a little worn, with accents that are stained a deep, royal purple. Strive for a life that has been used by God. A life that displays His fruitfulness.

Emily

Greater glory

*The glory of this present house will be greater
than the glory of the former house.*
Haggai 2:9 NIV

When Solomon's magnificent Temple replaced the Tabernacle, it became the place in which God's glory dwelt. But as the Israelites spiraled downward into sin and idolatry, God's righteous judgment fell upon them. God allowed the Babylonians to pillage, destroy and, ultimately, to burn down the Temple and take the Israelite people into captivity. They even captured the ark of the covenant which housed the physical presence of God.

Seventy years later, the impoverished exiles of Israel returned to their land and rebuilt the Temple under Zerubbabel's rule. This Temple (often called Zerubbabel's Temple) was erected during a time of great economic depression; it could not even be compared with the ornately embellished, expensively adorned Temple Solomon had built.

But even though the new Temple did not contain the precious ark, God reminded the Israelites that His invisible presence was with them, and that He was pleased and glorified by their obedience in rebuilding the Temple. God's sweetest encouragement to them, however, was this promise in Haggai. God promised that Zerubbabel's Temple would one day enjoy far greater glory than even Solomon's spectacular sanctuary.

Sure enough, several hundred years later, greater glory came as a carpenter and his young wife entered that temple. In their arms, they held their firstborn—a son. Few recognized God's glory that day as the tiny infant was dedicated. Nevertheless, God had kept His promise. Greater glory had come indeed.

Laurie

Wait while you wait

*I wait for the Lord, my whole being waits,
and in his word I put my hope.*
Psalm 130:5 NIV

Submitting to God's timing can leave you feeling a little lost, like maybe your whole life is on hold until the miraculous moment in which God finally says, "Now." When we're waiting on God's perfect timing, we sometimes become like little children sitting in the backseat of a car asking God, "Are we there yet?" with every turn. That kind of response can make for a very long journey.

Instead, one of the best things you can do as you wait on God is to wait on God. It sounds circular, but remember that there are two different definitions of "to wait." One implies sitting quietly, not doing anything until an appointed time. The other implies serving someone; to wait on someone as a waitress serves her customers. You can and should wait on (serve) God as you wait on Him.

Emily

September 21

He will

For in the day of trouble he will keep me safe in his dwelling;
he will hide me in the shelter of his sacred tent
and set me high upon a rock.
Psalm 27:5 NIV

As you read today's Psalm, consider the two phrases that begin with the words "He will." Now take a moment to re-read this verse allowing the truth of that tiny two-word phrase to spiritually sink in.

What trouble, what problem, what stressful situation are you facing today? Prayerfully pour your heart out before God, then place your faith in His promise that He will.

Laurie

To know Christ

*I want to know Christ and experience the
mighty power that raised him from the dead.
I want to suffer with him, sharing in his death.*
Philippians 3:10 NLT

For some reason, when you suffer, it feels as if you're closer to Jesus than other times. There is comfort in knowing that He understands what it is to suffer.

The goal of our faith is not to eradicate suffering. It is not to eliminate all problems. It isn't even to get a happy ending. The goal of our faith is what Paul shares in Philippians: to know Christ. And sometimes, only in an experience full of deep pain will you be able to connect with Him more completely.

Laurie

Get the prize

> *Do you not know that in a race all the*
> *runners run, but only one gets the prize?*
> *Run in such a way as to get the prize.*
> I Corinthians 9:24 NIV

In the New Testament, the Christian life is often referred to as a race, yet so many times we set out to complete the course the Lord has placed in front of us with the same kind of flippancy one would demonstrate if she attempted to run a marathon without training first. We don't survey the big picture. We fail to set up recognizable goals and we are often at best apathetic about our efforts.

We should approach our spiritual growth with no less thought or consideration than we do our career goals, our weight-loss goals or our goals for saving for retirement. Don't set out for a leisurely jog when you've been dropped into a race for your life. Run in such a way as to get the prize!

Emily

Bless even them

Bless those who persecute you.
Don't curse them; pray that God will bless them.
Romans 12:14 NLT

If you really want to practice forgiveness, start blessing those who have hurt you. Bless them by doing good for them, saying good things about them and even thinking good about them. Then pray that God would bless them as well. You'll find that forgiveness takes on a whole new dimension and you will find yourself growing and maturing.

Laurie

A perfect lunch

Here is a boy with five small barley loaves and two small fish,
but how far will they go among so many?
John 6:9 NIV

We all know the story of how Jesus took a little boy's lunch and used it to perform one of the best-known miracles in the Bible—the feeding of over five thousand people. We've heard the story a hundred times and love the boy's willingness to share and the lesson in faith that the disciples learned that day.

But we often forget that behind the loaves and fishes was a mama who packed a lunch. It just so happened that on that particular day, God used that lunch for His glory. But she probably packed dozens, if not hundreds, of other lunches that were just, well, lunches.

So why was this mediocre, off-balanced, no-theme lunch so perfect? Because it could be used by God.

Your child may go through an entire twelve years of school with ordinary lunches. The question is will he be prepared for that one time when God chooses to turn his lunch into a miracle? Your job is not to force perfect moments upon your child by outdoing yourself with artwork and poetry and organic, thematic, musical, color-coordinated delicacies.

Your job is just to prepare your child to be used by God. And if that happens to be through a lunch, well then, you can always pin it on Pinterest.

Emily

Red flags

*Next Paul and Silas traveled through the area of Phrygia
and Galatia, because the Holy Spirit had prevented them
from preaching the word in the province of Asia at that times.*
Acts 16:6 NLT

Paul and Silas didn't know what was going on in the spiritual realm in Acts 16, but they did know one thing: they didn't have peace about going into Asia to share the gospel. For some reason, the Holy Spirit gave them a red flag and forbade them from preaching there at that time.

Colossians 3:15 says, "Let the peace of Christ rule in your hearts" (NIV). Decisions can be difficult, and sometimes we have no guidance other than peace or a lack of peace to move ahead on a decision. What decisions are you facing today? If you don't have the peace of God in your heart, you need to wait. That uneasiness is the Holy Spirit throwing you a red flag. Pay attention to those red flags now and you can avoid regret later.

Laurie

Grief and ministry

*Praise be to the God and Father of our Lord Jesus Christ,
the Father of compassion and the God of all comfort, who
comforts us in all our troubles, so that we can comfort those
in any trouble with the comfort we ourselves receive from God.*

2 Corinthians 1:3-4 NIV

One of the main reasons that God allows us to go through grief is so that we may have empathy for others who experience grief as well. Grief leads to ministry.

However, in order to comfort others in their troubles, never forget that you must first be comforted in yours. Allow God to comfort you through His Spirit. Receive His compassion. Use whatever time it takes to work through your hard times and do not rush it.

God can and will use your empathy to comfort others, but you must never skip over the grief and jump straight into the ministry.

Emily

His way

But passing through their midst, He went His way.
Luke 4:30 NASB

Jesus created quite a ruckus when He went to his boyhood home of Nazarath and read from the scrolls of Isaiah in the synagogue. The religious leaders considered it blasphemy that He would read a messianic prophecy and then say, "Today this Scripture has been fulfilled" (v. 21). They recognized His claim to be the Messiah and were so infuriated by it, they took Him to a hill where they intended to throw Him off a cliff.

But Jesus was not threatened by what others thought. When He got up on that hill, He didn't do what a lot of us would have done. He didn't apologize, He didn't back-peddle and He didn't let them destroy Him. Instead, He went *His* way. He went God's way. And because He knew who He was, He knew He would one day die on a hill, but it would not be that hill and it would not be that day.

Laurie

Be still

The Lord will fight for you;
you need only to be still.
Exodus 14:14 NIV

We know we should pray without ceasing. We like to put on the armor of God. We want to march like Joshua around our own personal Jerichos and take up our cross like Jesus commanded. Though we know the battle has already been won, we are eager to be victorious along the way!

But in the midst of the fighting, praying, marching and doing, we forget about one of the most effective battle strategies of all— the art of being still. "Be still, and know that I am God," He says in Psalm 46:10. "Be still and I will do the fighting for you!" He says in Exodus. Being still is difficult. It seems so unproductive. So pointless. So anti-Christian even. But when it comes to fighting a spiritual battle, there is victory in simply being still before the Lord.

Emily

You are what you wear

Since God chose you to be the holy people he loves,
you must clothe yourselves with tenderhearted mercy,
kindness, humility, gentleness, and patience.
Colossians 3:12 NLT

There's nothing wrong with caring about how you look or taking care of yourself. However, if you find yourself spending inordinate amounts of time, energy, thought or money on your outward appearance, you may need to rethink your "wardrobe."

Focusing too much on self-image can be a deadly sin for women because it switches the object of your worship from God to self. God wants you to focus more on your inside than on your outside. He doesn't care if you're dressed in the latest fashions from Paris, but He cares tremendously if you're clothed with mercy, kindness, gentleness and patience. Take care of your outward appearance, but never at the expense of your inner heart.

Laurie

october

A political warning

The LORD has given me a strong warning not to think like everyone else does. He said, "Don't call everything a conspiracy, like they do, and don't live in dread of what frightens them. Make the LORD of Heaven's Armies holy in your life. He is the one you should fear. He is the one who should make you tremble. He will keep you safe."
Isaiah 8:11-14 NLT

Whether it's an election year or not, politicians and commentators of all political persuasions constantly try to make you think like they think. And one of the primary tactics they will use is fear. Fear of the future. Fear of a worsening economy. Fear of your future health and welfare. Fear of energy costs and environmental disasters. And of course, fear of war.

But as a Christian, there's only one thing you should fear: God. And the God you fear has promised to keep you safe. So, as you read today's headlines, listen to the radio, or watch the news, don't be bullied to think like they think and fear what they fear. Let early voting begin today. Cast your vote for God. Trust Him. Believe Him. Fear Him. And He will keep you safe both before and after all elections because (unlike most politicians) He *always* keeps His promises.

Laurie

Understanding

Jesus replied, "You do not realize now what I am doing,
but later you will understand."
John 13:7 NIV

With Jesus, we have the promise of understanding. What does this mean, exactly? This means that everything might not make sense right now, but someday it will! That "someday" might not be until we're in Heaven and talking to Jesus face to face, but someday we will see that the chaos we experienced, the questions we screamed, and the confusion we felt were all being held together by a loving, organized, master planner who was weaving our lives for His glory.

Is God confusing to you? Are you having trouble understanding why He's not acting faster or slower or nicer or just differently? Understanding will come. Right now, you see just a puzzle piece when God sees the whole puzzle. You see what's happening on stage while God sees what's happening in the wings. You see the underside of a tapestry when God sees the upper.

You may not realize now what He is doing, but later you will understand.

Emily

October 3

Planting seeds

It is the same with my word. I send it out,
and it always produces fruit. It will accomplish all I want it to,
and it will prosper everywhere I send it.
Isaiah 55:10-11 NLT

The Bible says that God's Word does not return void. It may feel like your words, your encouragement, your songs, or your prayers are falling on deaf ears when you try to share God's Word with some people, especially with small children. But even when you think they aren't listening, seeds are still being planted.

So if you're feeling frustrated that your kids, co-workers or students are completely ignoring you when it comes to all things spiritual, remember God's promise. His Word does not return void. You may have moments when someone tunes you out and you think it's hopeless, but just remember to keep planting those seeds anyway. In His perfect time, you'll begin to see fruit.

Emily

Sing a song

*Be filled with the Spirit, speaking to one another with psalms,
hymns, and songs from the Spirit. Sing and make music
from your heart to the Lord.*
Ephesians 5:18–19 NIV

Do you have a song in your heart? When you sing, your unconscious melodies are really just the overflow of the ongoing song within your heart. So don't let that song remain silent any longer! Sing! Give expression to the song He has placed within your heart. In your car, in the aisles of the grocery store, and especially in your home, sing. Audibly or inaudibly. Consciously or subconsciously. As the Spirit leads you, sing. Sure, you may occasionally annoy a teenager, and you may even experience the stares of strangers. But you will also glorify God. And never forget: as His temple, that's what you're here for. So sing, and you're sure to start *glo*-ing, girl!

Laurie

Fruit, not fruits

But the fruit of the Spirit is love, joy, peace, forbearance,
kindness, goodness, faithfulness, gentleness and self-control.
Against such things there is no law.
Galatians 5:22-23 NIV

Many people misquote Galatians 5:22 by making it plural. They say the *fruits* of the Spirit instead of the *fruit* of the Spirit. However, *fruit* is singular, and that one distinction is significant in understanding how to produce healthy spiritual fruit.

You don't get healthy fruit by watering the fruit itself. Instead, you water the roots and the fruit will flourish. Likewise, spiritual fruit is not produced by concentrating on the growth of specific fruit, like trying to have more joy, more peace or more self-control, but by focusing on the root of the issue, which is keeping "in step with the Spirit" (v. 25) and maintaining overall spiritual health. Maintain the roots and the fruit will follow.

10/5/15 –

Emily

Flattery versus rebuke

*Whoever rebukes a person will in the end gain favor
rather than one who has a flattering tongue.*
Proverbs 28:23 NIV

Which is more valuable—a sweet-talking man, or a friend who tells you when you have a huge piece of broccoli stuck in your teeth?

As women, we all love to hear someone say, "You look really good today!" And there's nothing wrong with receiving a compliment about your appearance. But use discretion when it comes to the things you hear. Consider the source. Consider the subject. Flattery may be easier to hear, but a gentle rebuke from someone who loves you is far more helpful.

4/15 - Emily rebuking Kerry Oglesby.

Emily

Self-righteousness

You must have the same attitude that Christ Jesus had.
Though he was God, he did not think of equality with God
as something to cling to. Instead, he gave up his
divine privileges; he took the humble position
of a slave and was born as a human being.
Philippians 2:5-7 NLT

If you have children, especially teenagers, or if you have a husband who is not a Christian, self-righteousness can ruin your witness with them. When you know the truth of God's Word and you can see that those closest to you are not following it like you are, it can be tempting to take a judgmental or preachy approach with them. But beware girls. This self-righteous attitude makes us look, in other people's eyes, very ugly and that in turn makes us poor representatives and ambassadors for Christ.

Jesus is the only one who ever lived a perfect life on earth, but even He chose humility instead of arrogance in His relationship with others. When you flaunt what you perceive as your spiritual maturity, you will repel others away from the Lord instead of draw them closer to Him.

Laurie

Spiritually in sync

After David had finished talking with Saul,
Jonathan became one in spirit with David,
and he loved him as himself.
I Samuel 18:1 NIV

David and Jonathan are a perfect example of an unlikely friendship. Jonathan was King Saul's son, and technically in line for the throne, but David was God's choice to be the next king. Egos and agendas could have ruined these two forever, but because they were both devoted to the Lord, their friendship lasted through generations.

Do you have a friend who is spiritually in sync with you? One who encourages you to follow God's will and seek His best for your life? Such friends are rare and are a great blessing from the Lord. Thank God for that friend and then tell her how much she means to you.

Emily

Rise up!

But you belong to God, my dear children.
You have already won a victory over those people,
because the Spirit who lives in you is greater than
the spirit who lives in the world.
I John 4:4 NLT

The Immoral Woman hasn't just captured our culture. She's actively seducing the church as well. Using television, movies, magazines and the Internet, she seeks to desensitize us to her permissive, provocative lifestyle. She coaxes us to compromise our own standards and to give in to our daughters who protest and proclaim, "Mom, everybody dresses like this. It's no big deal. And besides, if a guy has a problem with the way I'm dressed, then he shouldn't be looking. Just because I'm a Christian doesn't mean I can't look hot."

Battle-weary moms unite! Married women, single women, old and young women alike, rise up! It's time to declare war on the aggressive, destructive, power-hungry presence of the Immoral Woman in our lives. We must arm ourselves with the Truth and send her back to the satanic pit she came from. And by the authority of God's Word I can promise you this: Victory is ours for the taking.

Laurie

Remembering the babies

He answered, "While the child was still alive,
I fasted and wept. I thought, 'Who knows?
The Lord may be gracious to me and let the child live.'
But now that he is dead, why should I go on fasting?
Can I bring him back again? I will go to him,
but he will not return to me."
2 Samuel 12:22-23 NIV

After David and Bathsheba's first son died, David found comfort in the fact that he would see his son again in Heaven. If you've experienced losing a child from miscarriage, stillbirth, abortion or infant death, you know that it doesn't matter if it's been one week or thirty years, you will never forget your sweet baby.

With two miscarriages in my past, I am thankful for David's words in 2 Samuel, and I am also thankful that October is National Pregnancy and Infant Loss Awareness Month. It's not only a chance to remember my babies that I never got to know; it's also a chance to reach out to other mothers who share this silent grief with me.

On one hand, I grieve the lives that ended too soon. But on the other, I rejoice for them. When I think of those babies, safe in the arms of Jesus, I get excited for them! How wonderful to bypass this fallen world and go directly to Paradise! How blessed they are to see Jesus face to face! How we wish they could return to us, but how wonderful it will be when we can go to them!

Emily

Saying no

*As Jesus was getting into the boat, the man who
had been demon possessed begged to go with him.
But Jesus said, "No, go home to your family,
and tell them everything the Lord has done
for you and how merciful he has been."*
Mark 5:18-19 NLT

Is it difficult for you to tell people "No"? What if you know they are well-meaning? What if you know it will hurt their feelings?

Telling people "No" is difficult, especially if you're a people-pleaser. But even Jesus had to set boundaries. I imagine that after being healed from demon possession, the man in Mark 5 was being genuine, grateful and insistent when he begged Jesus to go with Him into His boat. But Jesus knew something that the man didn't know. He knew that if the man was to come with Him, His own ministry would be derailed.

Telling someone "No" may not be easy, but if you let other people hijack your life, not only will you not be able to follow God's will for your life, they won't be able to fulfill God's will for their lives either. Do yourself—and them—a favor. Be a God-pleaser instead of a people-pleaser.

Laurie

Chase purity

*Finally, brothers and sisters, whatever is true,
whatever is noble, whatever is right, whatever is pure,
whatever is lovely, whatever is admirable—
if anything is excellent or praiseworthy—
think about such things.*
Philippians 4:8 NIV

The Bible says to "Flee from sexual immorality" (1 Cor. 6:18 NIV). Obviously, that is wonderful advice. Sometimes, however, it's difficult to run *away* from something unless you have something specific to run *towards*.

In the case of sexual immorality, the best way to flee from it is to run towards its opposite. Run towards moral things. Chase purity. It is impossible to run towards purity and immorality at the same time, so run after purity by always thinking about the things of God. Think about His holiness. Immerse yourself in His Word. Surround yourself with television shows, books and relationships that are morally uplifting. If you're intentional about chasing purity, you will automatically have your back towards immorality which makes fleeing that much easier.

Emily

Invest in rest

> *For in six days the Lord made the heavens,*
> *the earth, the sea, and everything in them;*
> *but on the seventh day he rested.*
> *That is why the Lord blessed the*
> *Sabbath day and set it apart as holy.*
> Exodus 20:11 NIV

Never underestimate the value of quality rest. God rested after creation. He established the Sabbath day as a day of rest for His people. And even Jesus withdrew from the crowds frequently to get alone and rest in the presence of His Father.

You need rest too. Resting allows you to recharge and to be more productive in the long run. So work like the dickens while you're "on the clock," but rest guilt-free when you can.

Emily

Wisdom, knowledge and truth

For wisdom will enter your heart,
and knowledge will fill you with joy.
Proverbs 2:10 NLT

As you can see by today's Proverb, the old "ignorance is bliss" philosophy is a lie. In fact, Jesus said, "You shall know the truth, and the truth shall make you free" (John 8:32 NASB).

Spend a few moments in prayer thanking God for the wisdom, knowledge, and truth He's given you through His liberating, life-changing Word.

Laurie

Follow the leader

Then the people complained and turned against Moses.
Exodus 15:24 NLT

After the spiritual high of crossing the Red Sea, the Israelites' first problem was that they began to doubt their God-ordained leader. Sure Moses was good enough to lead them across dry land, but was he good enough to keep them from dying of thirst? (Exodus 15:22-25).

God places leaders in your life in order to help you follow Him. They come in the form of pastors, teachers, parents or mentors. Look at the spiritual leaders in your life. What do they have to offer you? Are you milking them for their wisdom? Now is the time to review your sermon notes. Re-read those Bible passages. Listen to that CD. Find out what resources are available to you and maximize on them.

Emily

Without fault

*Even before he made the world, God loved us and chose us
in Christ to be holy and without fault in his eyes.*
Ephesians 1:4 NLT

Self-abasement is the constant need to live in a pit of guilt and shame instead of moving forward in the victory you have through Christ. It keeps you from getting past your past even though the Lord has already forgiven you. Do you constantly lament the wasted moments, wasted days, or wasted years in your past? Do you feel like a second class Christian and useless in God's kingdom?

If you are a Christian, you are without fault in God's eyes. But, are you without fault in your own eyes as well?

Laurie

Power to forgive

> *"But that you may know that the Son of Man has power on earth*
> *to forgive sins"—He said to the man who was paralyzed,*
> *"I say to you, arise, take up your bed, and go to your house."*
> Luke 5:24 NIV

You may think that certain sins are so great that there's no way that God could ever forgive them. They're too bad. They're too dark. They're too unthinkable. Certainly God's holiness would prevent Him from pardoning such despicable behavior.

We forget that God's forgiveness is a reflection of His power. The question is not how big the sin is, but how big God is. Is God smaller than your sin? Is He so powerless that He can't forgive something? Certainly not.

Emily

Live in harmony

Live in harmony with each other. Don't be too proud to enjoy the company of ordinary people. And don't think you know it all!
Romans 12:16 NLT

Even in a church setting, there may be many areas of disagreement. Opinions may conflict and personalities may clash. But in those times when disagreements are on matters that are theologically nonessential, harmony should be your goal, not being right. Not getting your way. Not setting everybody straight.

There may be a lot of things that we as believers disagree on. But we should disagree in a way that builds one another up. Our aim should be harmony. Our goal, unity.

Laurie

Not my glory

> *When I consider your heavens, the work of your fingers,*
> *the moon and the stars, which you have set in place,*
> *what is mankind that you are mindful of them,*
> *human beings that you care for them?*
> Psalm 8:3-4 NIV

Has God ever surprised you? Has He ever given you a front row seat to a miracle? Have His blessings ever left you in awe? Have you ever wondered, as David did, "Why in the world does the God of the universe allow little ole me to have purpose in His infinite plans?"

It is humbling, to say the least, but it happens.

He uses housewives and teachers and grandmothers and cashiers. He blesses children and lawyers and custodians and waiters. His blessings are color blind, gender neutral, and do not discriminate against age, height, weight or hair color.

All He looks for is a willing, obedient heart.

And when He finds that in you, and blesses or uses you to a degree that brings you to your knees in humility, sometimes the only response you can utter is, "Not my glory, but Yours."

Emily

Belt of truth

Stand firm then, with the belt of truth buckled around your waist.
Ephesians 6:14 NIV

A good belt, no matter what it looks like, keeps your shirt from flying up and your pants from falling down. It holds your entire outfit together and keeps you from being, well, naked. The belt of truth works in the same way.

When God's truth is central in our lives, it keeps us from being exposed, vulnerable, and naked around the enemy. Without truth, our pants slip down and puddle around our feet leaving us to trip over our own shoes, whether they're shod with the gospel of peace or not. Without truth, the breastplate of righteousness inches up our chests like a baby doll dress in a windstorm, leaving our most vital organs exposed and unguarded. Without truth, our only weapon has no place to lock in by our side, and the sword of the Spirit clanks to the ground out of reach and out of commission.

Truth is more than just an accessory to the armor of God. Truth is what holds the armor of God together.

Emily

I know that there is nothing better for them than to rejoice…
Ecclesiastes 3:12 NASB

There comes a time when everyone feels a little crazy. Unhinged. Loony. Cuckoo. Bananas. Or just downright insane.

If you're feeling a little "nuts-o" today, take the first step on your road back to sanity by praising the Lord. Thank Him for all that He's given you (salvation, eternal life, peace, and even kids, co-workers and family members who sometimes make you crazy).

As you purposely focus on God, rejoicing will supernaturally enable you to rise above your pathetic pity party and even your worst martyr moments.

Laurie

Do good

...and to do good in one's lifetime....
Ecclesiastes 3:12 NASB

After you've rejoiced and praised God for the person or situation that is making you lose your mind, turn your thoughts into actions by doing good.

It may be hard, but you need to love the unlovable (even warring siblings, disobedient children and contentious co-workers). Doing good may involve performing an undeserved act of kindness or it may mean correcting and disciplining those under your authority without yelling.

Don't expect your nice gestures to go rewarded or even acknowledged. Just do good for the sake of doing good. Your sanity will slowly begin to return.

Laurie

See good

> ...moreover, that every man who eats and drinks
> sees good in all his labor—it is the gift of God.
> Ecclesiastes 3:13 NASB

If your sanity is still slipping and you're ready to quit your job, run away from home, or eat your weight in cookie dough, continue your quest for sanity by choosing to see good.

Review helpful Scriptures like Romans 8:28, Philippians 1:6, and James 1:2-4. Write them on sticky notes and refer to them throughout the day. Plaster your 'fridge, make-up mirror, pantry door or desk with the encouraging Word of God to help you to see good when life's, well, not so good.

Laurie

Fear God

I know that everything God does will remain forever;
there is nothing to add to it and there is nothing to take from it,
for God has so worked that men should fear Him.
Ecclesiastes 3:14 NASB

Your flesh wants you to deal with stress by getting loud and telling someone off, by heading to the mall and running up your credit cards or by giving up and giving in to depression and hopelessness. But when you fear God, you can resist your flesh by submitting to His sovereignty over your circumstances. When you fear God, you'll also discover that you have the strength to stand up to your flesh and say, "Stop messing with me because I'm going to walk in the Spirit."

When you feel like you're losing your mind, a healthy fear of the Lord can stop you from doing something you'll regret later. Something that will make your problems worse instead of better. If you want to keep from pulling your hair out, rejoice, do good, see good, and finally, fear God.

Laurie

Loyalty, not logistics

But Moses said, "Pardon your servant, Lord.
Please send someone else."
Exodus 4:13 NIV

When the Lord called Moses to lead the Israelites out of Egypt, Moses was quick with excuses and slow with obedience. "Who am I?" he asked. "Suppose *this* happens? What if *that* happens? Have you thought about *this* problem?" Each time, the Lord answered his questions and caused his excuses to melt into nothingness. Finally though, the truth behind Moses' questions came out. "Please send someone else." For Moses, it was never about uncertainties. It was about unwillingness.

What is the Lord calling you to do? What questions do you have? What excuses are you giving? If the Lord is asking you to do something, focus only on your loyalty to Him, not on the logistics of the mission.

Emily

God is love

*Whoever does not love does not know God,
because God is love.*
I John 4:8 NIV

God is love. It may be the very first thing that you learned about Him. Before you learned that He created you, before you learned that He sent His son, before you learned that He has a plan for your life, you probably sang this: "Jesus loves me, this I know. For the Bible tells me so."

Yes, God loves you, but God also is love. So He is able to love you with the purest, most powerful, most eternal type of love there is. It's a type of love reserved only for Him because He is the only One who is capable of such love.

His love has no strings attached, no conditions and no limits. And while it costs you nothing, never forget that it cost Him everything.

Emily

October 27

Finish the race

> However, I consider my life worth nothing to me,
> if only I may finish the race and complete the task
> the Lord Jesus has given me—the task of
> testifying to the gospel of God's grace.
> Acts 20:24 NIV

Sometimes we fall short of the finish line because we fail to formulate recognizable milestones along the way. We reach for intangible things like the fruit of the spirit (love, joy, peace, patience, kindness, goodness, faithfulness, gentleness and self-control; Gal. 5:22-23 NIV) but fail to convert those aspirations into measurable goals. We reach for peace but neglect to walk away from a situation or person that causes turmoil. We want to become kind but fail to translate that into everyday menial tasks. We aspire to have self-control, then wonder why we can't stop reaching for the thing we've neglected to put out of sight.

Be deliberate and intentional about your race to the finish line. Then you will be able to say, like Paul, "I have fought the good fight, I have finished the race, I have kept the faith" (2 Tim. 4:7 NIV).

Emily

Glo: 365 Devotions to Give God Priority

Rebuilding the temple

*In the last days the mountain of the Lord's temple
will be established as the highest of the mountains;
it will be exalted above the hills, and all nations will stream to it.*
Isaiah 2:2 NIV

After Christ's death, the prophecy He made regarding the temple was fulfilled. In 70 AD the Romans stormed Jerusalem, set fire to Herod's Temple, and destroyed it completely. Since that time a Jewish temple has never been rebuilt.

Instead, in the seventh century, another structure was erected on the former temple site. This structure is the Mosque of Omar, more commonly referred to as "The Dome of the Rock." It was built by the Muslims to commemorate their prophet, Muhammad. Tragically the large gold dome of a false religion has now become the dominant feature of Jerusalem's landscape.

You may be wondering, "Will another temple ever be built?" Yes, the Scriptures teach that there will be a temple during the millennial reign of Christ and that the nations will come and worship there (Isa. 2:2–4, Ezek. 40–43, Zech. 14). Until then, however, remember that "your body is a temple of the Holy Spirit" (1 Cor. 6:19 NASB).

Laurie

Love and discipline

Those whom I love I rebuke and discipline.
Revelation 3:19 NIV

It's never fun to be on the receiving end of discipline, but it's also hard to be on the giving end as well. Any parent who's ever found himself saying, "This is going to hurt me more than it hurts you," understands the dilemma. There is a part of you that wants to skip over the punishment phase of your child's rebellion and jump straight to the part where the lesson has been learned and the behavior has been corrected.

But the Bible is clear that to love someone is to discipline him. And if that feels unpleasant for a parent, imagine how God feels when He has to discipline us. But He does it anyway because He loves us. And His discipline has a very specific purpose—it leads to our holiness.

Perhaps you're in the middle of a difficult time right now and you're wondering why God doesn't just help you skip over it. Could it be that your trials are the result of some poor choices and that God is merely letting you face the consequences of your actions? If so, know that He is more concerned with your holiness than anything else, and that the discipline you are going through is a reflection of His love for you.

Emily

Build him up

*Do not let any unwholesome talk come out of your mouths,
but only what is helpful for building others up according
to their needs, that it may benefit those who listen.*
Ephesians 4:29 NIV

No matter how long you've been married, marriage will always be work. However, it will also always be worth the work.

It may take work to filter your speech with your husband. It may be difficult to swallow unwholesome talk and speak only what will be helpful in building him up. But you must learn to affirm and appreciate your husband verbally. Notice and compliment his positive attributes. Encourage his strengths. Do not take for granted that he knows how much he is appreciated. Your marriage will never come to a point where you can go on cruise control. He needs to hear encouragement from you today, tomorrow and "'til death do you part."

Laurie

Light has come

This is the judgment, that the Light has come into the world,
and men loved the darkness rather than the Light,
for their deeds were evil.

John 3:19 NASB

Within the heart of every single one of us is the desire to know our Creator. God Himself implanted that desire. He wants us to want to know Him. And from the beginning of creation, God has made Himself known. He has not concealed Himself from His creation. He has not masked Himself in mysticism. He is not veiled within eastern meditation, and He is not attained by achieving a higher degree of consciousness. In fact, God wants the world to know Him so much that He sent His one and only Son into the world to save the world (John 3:16–17).

God has done everything possible in order that we may know Him. But the truth is: "Light has come into the world, but men loved darkness rather than the Light" (John 3:19). God has given us countless opportunities to know Him through the light of His Son, through the light of His Word, and through the light of His reflection in the lives of His children. But sadly, many still prefer darkness.

When you're surrounded by like-minded people, it's easy to forget that not everyone prefers the Light. The only true and lasting cure for the darkness in our world today is the light of Jesus Christ, and you should be more committed than ever before to allow the glorious light of Christ to shine through your everyday life.

Emily

november

Being thankful

*Through Jesus, therefore, let us continually offer to God
a sacrifice of praise—the fruit of lips that openly profess his name.
And do not forget to do good and to share with others,
for with such sacrifices God is pleased.*
Hebrews 13:15-16 NIV

Being thankful is an art, not a science; nevertheless, the Bible does help us understand how to maintain a spirit of thanksgiving. First, thanksgiving should be a sincere and spontaneous fruit that naturally occurs as a result of the condition of your heart. Only apples can grow from an apple tree. Likewise, if you want your lips to produce the fruit of thanksgiving, you must nurture the roots of thanksgiving in your heart.

Thanksgiving is also a sacrifice. Sometimes it is not easy. Sometimes it costs you greatly. You may have to set aside anger or bitterness in order to give sincere praise. But God is pleased when you sacrifice your praise, even if you must do it on a broken altar.

Finally, thanksgiving should be shared with others. Do not keep the Lord's provisions to yourself. Share them often. Thanksgiving, when shared, multiplies.

Emily

Not ashamed

The Lord God has opened My ear; And I was not disobedient,
Nor did I turn back… For the Lord God helps Me, Therefore,
I am not disgraced; Therefore, I have set My face like flint,
And I know that I will not be ashamed.
Isaiah 50:5, 7 NASB

The Lord has a call on your life, and if you want to follow His way, you must not only discern His call but also act upon it. Is the Lord speaking to you? You've heard and you know what you're supposed to do it, but you're hesitant. "What will other people think? If I do that, it's going to ruffle some feathers. If I do that, I'm going to have to tell some people no."

One day, you're going to stand before the One who has called you and if you have followed His call, you are not going to be ashamed. Until then, people may ridicule you. They may even be upset with you. But one day, if you follow Him, there will be no shame. There will be only joy and rejoicing because you've followed Him.

Laurie

November 3

After amen

Never will I leave you; never will I forsake you.
Hebrews 13:5 NIV

Have you ever felt worse instead of better after praying? It's unsettling, uncomfortable and the exact opposite of how you want to feel after praying.

After amen, you want to feel peace, comfort, and encouragement. But when those feelings fail to appear, you can be very hard on yourself. You can blame yourself, conclude that you must be praying incorrectly and commit to try harder next time. But that is a pointless cycle that never leads to the comfort you long to feel.

Instead, if you want to feel better instead of worse after praying, you must:

- Accept the fact that faith and feelings don't always go together.
- Choose faith over feelings.
- Move forward by faith without the feelings.

To "move forward by faith," you keep doing what you've been doing: praying, spending time in God's Word, walking in obedience, and clinging to the truth that God will never leave you or forsake you.

Even on your worst days, God says—no, He promises—that He is with you. And this remains true whether you feel anything or not. Feelings are unreliable and untrustworthy. God, on the other hand, is faithful. Forever. And unlike feelings, He never changes.

What will you do after amen?

Laurie

Natural beauty

Charm is deceptive, and beauty is fleeting;
but a woman who fears the Lord is to be praised.
Proverbs 31:30 NIV

With enough makeup, almost anyone can look physically beautiful. What's harder to find is someone who is a natural beauty. Someone who looks great in sweats, a ponytail, and *no* makeup! Those are the women who are truly physically beautiful, and there aren't many who fit that category.

Spiritual beauty works in the same way. Almost anyone can *look* spiritually beautiful by going to church, saying the "spiritual thing" at the right time, and participating in a service project or two. What's harder to find is someone who is a natural beauty spiritually. Someone who looks just as beautiful at home as she does in church. Someone who responds the same way to her difficult children or parents as she does to her pastor. Someone who uses the same language around her friends as she uses around her small group leader. The women who act, speak and think like Christ regardless of who is watching are the ones who are truly spiritually beautiful.

There's nothing wrong with taking care of yourself and trying to look nice. But at the end of the day, the hair comes down and the makeup washes down the sink. With spiritual "primping," however, anyone can become a natural beauty.

Emily

Bigger picture

Then Joseph said to his brothers, "Come close to me."
When they had done so, he said, "I am your brother Joseph,
the one you sold into Egypt! And now, do not be distressed
and do not be angry with yourselves for selling me here,
because it was to save lives that God sent me ahead of you.
Genesis 45:4-5 NIV

When Joseph was reunited with his brothers, he thought he understood God's purposes for allowing him to be sold into slavery over twenty years earlier. His position allowed him to provide food for his family and to save them from the famine.

You might think that the preservation of Joseph's family would be purpose enough for God to allow Joseph to endure and experience all that he did during those twenty-plus years he was in Egypt. But God's purposes exceeded that. God had a much bigger picture in mind when He sovereignly allowed Joseph to suffer and to succeed. God promised Abraham that he would make him into a great nation (Gen. 12:1-2), and generations later, Joseph was a key player in fulfilling that promise. (Gen. 47:27, Exod. 1:6-7).

God's purpose for you extends beyond your own life as well. He sees past your lifetime to the generations that will follow you.

Laurie

Gray hair optional

*These older women must train the younger women to love
their husbands and their children, to live wisely and be pure,
to work in their homes, to do good, and to be submissive to their
husbands. Then they will not bring shame on the word of God.*
Titus 2:4-5 NLT

I used to read this verse and imagine a footnote referring to a
"gray-hair clause" at the bottom of the page. The verse sank in
as "*old* women must train the *young* women" instead of "*older*
women must train the *younger* women." I thought you had to be
a seasoned grandmother before you could pass your wisdom to
the next generation.

But you don't have to be *old* in order to be *older*. You can be a
Titus 2 woman regardless of your age. When a younger girl
has questions about life, she probably won't submit an official
request for you to be her mentor. She'll probably just test the
waters through tidbits of conversation. So watch for those subtle
openings in everyday conversations and see how God gives you
opportunities to minister to those who are younger than you.

Emily

How He helps

Help us, O God of our salvation, for the glory of Your name;
And deliver us and forgive our sins for Your name's sake.
Psalm 79:9 NASB

One of the most glorious attributes of God is that He stoops to help us. Just think: the sovereign God and Creator of the universe desires to help you. Why? It's very simple: God helps you for the glory of His name. How has He helped you this week? Take a few minutes to prayerfully and specifically thank Him for the way He's helped you. Glorify His name in prayer right now.

Laurie

Praise God for your job

Lazy people want much but get little,
but those who work hard will prosper.
Proverbs 13:4 NLT

If you work outside the home, there may be times when you feel that it's impossible to honor God at work when you don't like your job. You may even shut down and resort to doing the bare minimum since no one appreciates you anyway.

It helps to remember, however, that your job, no matter how undesirable, is still a blessing from God. It may not pay enough, but it pays something. It may be difficult, but it's not impossible. It may not be your dream job, but it could be teaching you something you need for your future dream job.

The day may come when God moves you elsewhere, but until then, start thanking Him for your job, for the people you work with and for the benefits your job provides. The simple act of thanksgiving will make your job more enjoyable.

Emily

Who are you pleasing?

> *Our purpose is to please God, not people.*
> *He alone examines the motives of our hearts.*
> I Thessalonians 2:4 NLT

Some women live to please others. They base their decisions upon an unhealthy fear of what others will think. Ultimately, they remain immature in their faith and stunted in their spiritual growth.

However, wise women live to please God. They base their decisions upon a healthy fear of the Lord (Prov. 31:30) and obedience to Him. Ultimately, they become mature in their faith and "grow in the grace and knowledge of the Lord" (2 Pet. 3:18 NIV).

Who are you trying to please today? Your friends? Your boss? Your parents? Your husband? Your purpose is not to please them at all, but to please the One who matters: God. Make it your goal to please Him with the one thing that He wants more than anything else—obedience.

Laurie

Not how I would have done it

"For my thoughts are not your thoughts,
neither are your ways my ways," declares the Lord.
Isaiah 55:8 NIV

How many times have you read a story in the Bible and thought, "Well, that's not how I would have done it!"?

- Establish a nation through a barren, geriatric couple?
- Conquer a city by marching around it for seven days?
- Reduce an army of thousands to just 300 men?
- Allow the son of God to be born in a manger?
- Launch a church with a handful of fishermen, tax collectors and sinners?
- Give eternal life by dying on a cross?

That's not how I would have done it.

It seems God has a strange habit of avoiding the easy way. Instead of using the direct route from point A to point B, He leads us through detours, twists, turns, tangents, circles, hurdles, flip flops, obstacle courses and quicksand before we finally arrive at our destination disoriented and confused, but thankful nonetheless.

His ways may not be your ways, but when you trust God with the journey as well as the destination, you embrace the scenery, as scary as it may be, as an opportunity to draw even closer to God.

Emily

His presence

And [God] said, "My presence shall go with you,
and I will give you rest." Then [Moses] said to Him,
"If Your presence does not go with us,
do not lead us up from here."
Exodus 33:14-15 NASB

In the midst of difficult circumstances, Moses went to the place where he consistently met one-on-one with God. And when he entered, the people stood and watched as God's majestic presence descended in the form of a cloud upon a humble tent which housed within it a very humble man. That morning, as he went to the tent, Moses showed his people that his priority—in good times and in bad—was to seek God's presence. And that morning, by God's gracious example, the Lord revealed His desire to experience intimate fellowship with man. Suddenly, a day that had once looked hopeless became hopeful.

Moses knew something that far too many of us have either forgotten or have come to take for granted. Moses knew that God's presence is absolutely essential in every step we take and in every mile of every journey we make. Moses not only recognized that he desperately needed God's presence, he also recognized that he desperately depended upon God's presence in his day-to-day life. Do you?

Laurie

Behind judgment

But God demonstrates His own love toward us,
in that while we were yet sinners, Christ died for us.
Romans 5:8 NASB

If you haven't noticed, the Bible is violent! For example, there's more to Noah's ark than cute animals that go marching in two-by-two. It's about people perishing. People drowning. People dying because they had turned their backs on God. Abraham's sacrifice is about a father tying up his son and laying him on an altar, knife in hand and ready to take the next, unthinkable step. The Passover is about an angel of death sweeping in and killing the firstborn male of every household.

Death. Judgment. Violence. Sometimes it's hard to wrap your head around the fact that God was behind it all.

But the full story becomes easier to understand when you see that behind every act of violence, judgment, and death, God provides a way for life to continue.

- Behind the judgment of Noah's time was an ark, and then a rainbow. An escape. A new beginning. A promise.
- Behind Abraham was a ram caught in the thicket. A substitutionary sacrifice. A way out.
- Behind the angel of death was a Passover. A divine covering. An exemption from death.

Violent, yes. But redemptive, absolutely.

Although it's hard to accept God's judgment sometimes, and it's easy to scream, "Unfair! How could you? Why?!", it's also so refreshing to remember that God never judges without also providing grace. Because of our sin, we all deserve the death and destruction we see in the Old Testament stories. But God, in His infinite love for us, sent grace through Jesus instead.

Emily

High standards

Who may worship in your sanctuary, Lord?
Who may enter your presence on your holy hill?
Those who lead blameless lives and do what is right,
speaking the truth from sincere hearts.
Psalm 15:1-2 NIV

God's Word calls us to live consistent lives. Your beliefs should parallel the way you live. The God we profess to possess is holy, righteous and pure, therefore, the only way you can glorify Him is by living holy, righteous and pure lives. You cannot glorify God by compartmentalizing your spiritual life apart from your physical life.

God's standards for His children are high. When you look at your own fleshly abilities, it's easy to get disheartened by your weaknesses, shortcomings, and downright failures. But when you focus on Him and all that He's given you through the power of His indwelling Spirit, you are reminded, encouraged and confident that "He who began a good work in you will carry it on to completion until the day of Christ Jesus" (Phil. 1:6 NIV). Aren't you grateful for the promise of His Word!

Laurie

Pass the test

You have tested my thoughts and examined my heart in the night.
You have scrutinized me and found nothing wrong.
I am determined not to sin in what I say.
Psalm 17:3 NLT

This psalm by King David is the expression of one who diligently and purposefully sought to keep his heart pure. No, David was not perfect, but he was described as a man after God's own heart (1 Sam. 13:14). Become a woman after God's heart, and allow David's psalm to lead you into a time of prayer. Ask God to uncover any sin and wrong attitudes within your heart. Then quietly listen for His answer. Confess any sin before Him, and commit to making things right with others against whom you may have sinned. Continue in prayer until God has thoroughly examined your heart and until you know you can pass the "test," just as David said he could.

Laurie

It's a small world

*If that is how God clothes the grass of the field,
which is here today and tomorrow is thrown into the fire,
will he not much more clothe you—you of little faith?*
Matthew 6:30 NIV

Every year, Nikon hosts a photography contest called The Nikon Small World Photomicrography Competition. It's a competition that celebrates the beautiful combination of microscopes and photography. Scientists-turned-photographers from all over the world submit images of microscopic detail that no one would ever be able to see with the naked eye.

In 2011, the 2nd place photo that caught my eye was the beautiful, up-close photo of a simple blade of grass. When I saw the intricate, minute detail that lays within the microscopic nuances of such an ordinary, boring thing as a blade of grass, I was reminded of how much God cares about the small things.

You probably know that God has a purpose for your life. He sees the big picture and He knows your part in it. But did you know that He cares about the small things as well? He cares about your friendships, your struggles at work, your diet, your car trouble. All of it. So you don't have to reserve God for the big things in your life. He wants to be a part of the small things as well.

Emily

The author

> But know this first of all, that no prophecy of
> Scripture is a matter of one's own interpretation,
> for no prophecy was ever made by an act of human will,
> but men moved by the Holy Spirit spoke from God.
> 2 Peter 1:20-21 NASB

The Bible consists of the letters, poetry, and historical accounts of about forty different men. They had various professions, were different ages and lived in different time periods. Yet the theme, message and truth of every book of the Bible is miraculously consistent with the others and do not contradict each other.

God is the true author of His Word. Through the power of His Spirit, He inspired each and every word. Therefore, because He is a perfect and holy God, He cannot contradict Himself. He cannot say one thing on one page of His Word and then say an entirely different thing on the next page.

Laurie

In what do you hope?

> Woe to those who go down to Egypt for help, who rely on
> horses, who trust in the multitude of their chariots
> and in the great strength of their horsemen,
> but do not look to the Holy One of Israel,
> or seek help from the Lord.
>
> Isaiah 31:1 NIV

The Lord gave the Israelites four warnings through the prophet Isaiah. First, by telling them not to go down to Egypt, He was warning them not to depend on their *surroundings*. Second, by telling them not to rely on horses, He was warning them not to depend on their *stuff*. Third, when He said not to trust in a multitude of chariots, He was warning them against trusting in their *surplus*. And finally, He warned them not to depend on their own *strength* or on the strength of their army.

In what do you tend to place your hope? Your surroundings, your stuff, your surplus or your strength? The Lord says to woe to anyone who places their hope in anything but Him.

Emily

Whistle while you work

Sing the glory of His name; make His praise glorious!
Psalm 66:2 NIV

Did you know that God loves the sound of your voice, and He especially loves to hear you sing? Today, after you've spent some time in prayer, conclude your prayer with a solo of praise to the Lord. Sing any hymn or praise song the Holy Spirit impresses upon your heart. And don't worry about how you think your voice sounds. Just glorify Him with your voice, and continue to do so throughout the rest of your day. Feel free to hum, or sing or even whistle while you work today.

Laurie

November 19

Remember Egypt

*I am the LORD your God, who brought you
out of Egypt, out of the land of slavery.*
Exodus 20:2 NIV

You probably know the story about how Moses parted the Red Sea and led the Israelites out of Egypt and out of slavery. It's a story of adventure, suspense, deceit, supernatural events and supernatural provisions. In a way, it is the climax of the Old Testament.

But what you may not notice is that God never tires of reminding the Israelites of that event. "I am the LORD your God, who brought you out of Egypt, out of the land of slavery." This exact phrase occurs in the Bible around twenty times, and it almost becomes God's preferred title for Himself. By referring to Himself with such detail, He was reminding the Israelites that they could trust Him. He knew how forgetful they could be. He knows how forgetful *we* can be. If we don't make it a point to actively remember the things He has done for us, chances are, we'll forget.

Emily

Keep your distance

*And now, dear brothers and sisters, we give you
this command in the name of our Lord Jesus Christ:
Stay away from all believers who live idle lives and
don't follow the tradition they received from us.*
2 Thessalonians 3:6 NLT

When Paul commands us to stay away from believers who live idle lives, he is not telling us to turn our backs on them or to abandon them completely. But he is telling us to keep them at arm's length and to distance ourselves from their "problems."

This type of person knows how to spot the soft-hearted, full-of-mercy people in your church. They know that if they can just talk to them long enough or paint their circumstances out to be more dire than they really are, they can get what they want. And what they want it is to pull you in and make you feel sorry for them so that you will work more and they can work less. You may feel like you're exercising mercy when you help these people, but what you're really doing is encouraging laziness.

Laurie

Brace yourself

*Brace yourself like a man; I will question you,
and you shall answer me.*
Job 38:3 NIV

In the book of Job, we can see that this naïve expectation to fully understand God and His ways can fall upon even the most mature believers. Job went through a long, tedious time of suffering and trials, but he seemed to hold on to the fact that someday he would see clearly the reasoning behind the testing. Everywhere he looked, things seemed blurry and didn't make sense. He questioned God. He longed for understanding. And he expected that God would give him the clarity he so desired.

But when God finally answered Job, only one thing became perfectly clear: God did not owe Job a thing! No answers. No explanation. No clarity at all. In fact, He told Job that if anyone was qualified to ask the questions, it was He, not Job.

Emily

Praying for a sign

*Then Jesus told him, "Because you have seen me,
you have believed; blessed are those who
have not seen and yet have believed."*
John 20:29 NIV

Have you ever prayed for a sign before? Almost all of us have. The truth is, sometimes we get those signs that we pray for, like Gideon did in Judges 6, or like the sign of the rainbow in Genesis 9. But other times God asks us just to trust Him and believe, even when our eyes cannot see Him, our ears do not hear Him and our fingers cannot reach out and feel the evidence of His goodness.

Because we all go through times that God feels invisible or apathetic to us, we must prepare for those times in advance by strengthening our faith through His Word. How well do you really know what the Bible says about your God? Immerse yourself now in the truth of His Word so that the next time God seems invisible to you, the truth will eclipse any doubts you may have. You may still find yourself praying for a "sign," but don't be surprised when that sign is simply His Word manifesting itself clearly and lovingly into your heart.

Emily

As it depends on you

If possible, so far as it depends on you,
be at peace with all men.
Romans 12:18 NASB

Unfortunately, there are some people who do not like peace. Instead, they like conflict. They like being difficult. They enjoy the drama. Tension is just something they have learned to live with, so they love to get into it with any and everyone around them.

As Christians, we are supposed to "be at peace with all men," but there are some cases when you are off the hook. Yes, you should strive for peace with all people and seek reconciliation when you can. Yes, you should make sure you are not the source or cause of conflict. But, in those cases where you've done all you can do to be at peace and peace is still not accomplished, you need to rest in this verse. Sometimes, peace between two people simply is not possible. And when that is the case, you need to leave it up to God.

Laurie

Holy, holy, holy

*And they were calling to one another:
"Holy, holy, holy is the Lord Almighty;
the whole earth is full of his glory."*
Isaiah 6:3 NIV

Although describing God's divine holiness in human terms will always have its limitations, it helps to think of His holiness in three different ways:

- **Exclusiveness**. One definition of holy is *separate* or *exclusive*. When you say that God is holy, you're saying that He is so exclusive that no one else and nothing else is even in the same category as Him. He is beyond compare, has no equal and has no opposite.

- **Excellence**. His holiness is also used to encompass His moral excellence. Everything He does, thinks and speaks is right, good and perfect.

- **Exalted**. God's holiness makes Him worthy of praise. He does not acquire His holiness from someone else; He is innately and intrinsically holy in and of Himself. Because of this, He is to be exalted.

No wonder He has angels whose only purpose is to proclaim His holiness for all eternity.

Emily

Check your heart

As Solomon grew old, his wives turned his heart after other gods,
and his heart was not fully devoted to the Lord his God,
as the heart of David his father had been.
1 Kings 11:4 NIV

After a long period of peace, prosperity, and success as Israel's king, Solomon chose not to heed the warning God had given him to protect his heart and he married many foreign women. He had seen God's glory. He had heard God speak to him on several occasions and had God appear to him twice. Plus he had been blessed by God like no other man before him. But because he disobeyed God's command to protect his heart, he was led astray.

Who has access to your heart? Are they inching you closer to God, or are they turning you away from Him?

Laurie

New friends

A wise person wins friends.
Proverbs 11:30 NLT

Have you ever been around a group of new moms when they were talking about breast-feeding or potty training? Depending on your own stage of life, it can be the most liberating, encouraging conversation of the day, or it can be the most awkward and uncomfortable conversation of the day. You want and need friends who are in the same stage of life as you.

Understand that your life may move to the next stage according to a time-table different from your friend's. That's not cause to sever ties with her, but it is reason to consider adding to your circle of friends. If you're a new mom, reach out to other new moms. If you're recently retired, reach out to others who are retired as well. Pray that God will lead you to others who share your stage of life so that you can encourage each other to glorify Him in this shared season.

Emily

Love covers a multitude

Above all, love each other deeply,
because love covers over a multitude of sins.
1 Peter 4:8 NIV

If you're married, you probably know your husband's faults better than anyone. Maybe he leaves the toilet seat up. Maybe he spends too much money on golf. Maybe he forgets special dates. It would be extremely easy for you to focus or fixate on all of those little things he does that drive you crazy.

But that will never strengthen your marriage. Focusing on his shortcomings will not help him overcome them, and it will only drive him further away from you. Instead, let love cover his faults (even if they are a "multitude"), and most importantly, pray that he will do the same for you. Because whether or not you admit it, you have your own shortcomings and they need to be covered in love as well.

Laurie

Get in the Word?

If you remain in me and my words remain in you,
ask whatever you wish, and it will be done for you.
John 15:7 NIV

It's easy to run to the Bible for a quick fix when things are not going well. A verse here. A passage there. A little motivational pep talk to make it through the day. But God did not give us the Bible so that we could "get in the Word" whenever we need it. He gave it to us so that *His Word could get inside us*!

This is like the difference between taking antibiotics when you're sick and taking vitamins to keep from getting sick in the first place. The only way for God's Word to remain in you is to pro-actively *devour* it over a long period of time.

You may feel frustrated because you want God's Word rooted in you *now* and you wish you had started twenty years ago reading, memorizing and meditating. Don't fret. While the best time to plant an apple tree may be twenty years ago, the second best time is *today*.

Emily

Give good advice

I have good sense and give good advice.
I have understanding and power.
Proverbs 8:14 NIRV

You have influence. Whether it's with your friends, family, or fellow workers, your life influences others. Are you advising them wisely? Are you helping them succeed? Your responsibility as a woman of influence is huge. Get on your knees right now and ask God to give you wisdom in your relationships, conversations and dealings with others.

Laurie

Shout from the housetops

What I whisper in your ear,
shout from the housetops for all to hear!
Matthew 10:27 NLT

There are times to quietly ponder the intimate conversations you have with the Lord through His Word, but other times, you just need to SHOUT about what He is doing in your life! The peace you're feeling about upcoming change—share it with a friend. The hope you have after a family member's death—explain it to your children. The freedom you feel after accepting God's forgiveness—share it through your testimony.

When others see God's hand upon your life, it encourages them in their own lives. What is God whispering in your ear? Don't keep it a secret! SHOUT it out for all to hear!

Emily

December

Christmas sanity

*While they were there, the time came for the baby to be born,
and she gave birth to her firstborn, a son. She wrapped him
in cloths and placed him in a manger, because there was
no guest room available for them.*
Luke 2:6-7 NIV

The nativity. It's the secret to sanity at Christmastime. All of the Christmas clutter, the hectic holiday schedule, the to-do list and the to-buy list all become insignificant in the shadow of the true meaning of Christmas. As you look at each figurine of your nativity, the craziness disappears and joy and peace shine in its place.

This year, do not let a case of Christmas insanity rob you of the simplicity of the nativity. The most important thing you can do at Christmastime isn't decorating your house or shopping or baking or wrapping presents. The *most* important thing you can do at Christmas is worshiping Jesus and giving Him your best.

The nativity is a simple reminder that all of the other Christmas to-dos can wait. The secret to your Christmas sanity is on your mantel right in front of you.

Laurie

All smiles

*We always thank God for all of you and
continually mention you in our prayers.*
I Thessalonians 1:2 NIV

If you've ever tried to take a family photo, you probably remember the "outtakes." Behind the perfect poses and choreographed smiles that you share on your Christmas cards are the real moments. Moments of chaos, name-calling, hair-pulling, pushing, screaming and head-butting. And it's even worse when kids are involved!

The truth is that the photos people share on Christmas cards only tell part of the story, and there's only so much you can know about a person just by looking at her picture. Did she have a bad day today? Is her bank account laughing at her bills? Is her marriage in trouble? Is she just days away from a life-changing diagnosis from her doctor? Has she cried in the last 24 hours? Is she even on speaking terms with God?

This year, instead of taking the Christmas cards that you receive and throwing them in the trash or taping them to the mantel without a second thought, spend some time praying for each person or family in the pictures. You never know if behind the color-coordinated Christmas sweaters is a family in desperate need of God's favor.

Emily

December 3

God's mission for you

*He said to them, "Let us go somewhere else to the towns nearby,
so that I may preach there also; for that is what I came for."*
Mark 1:38 NASB

What are you here for? Jesus came to proclaim the gospel. He came to lay down His life as a ransom for all of us. He came and He did what God called Him to do. He had a mission and He was going to accomplish it.

But no matter where He went, it seemed that people were trying to steer Him off course. Some tried to derail Him with evil intentions because they didn't believe in Him, but others tried to derail Him with *good* intentions. One crowd of people found Jesus after He had healed many people in their village. They begged Him to stay with them because they believed He was the Messiah. Nevertheless, He remained true to His mission. "I must preach the Good News of the Kingdom of God in other towns, too, because that is why I was sent" (Luke 4:43 NLT).

What is God's mission for you? Accomplishing it means that sometimes you may have to turn people down, even if they have nothing but good intentions.

Laurie

Change your focus

I will sing the Lord's praise, for he has been good to me.
Psalm 13:6 NIV

Our difficult circumstances are magnified when we focus on them. Small problems grow larger. Inconveniences become impossibilities. Obstacles become roadblocks. But when we focus on God instead of our circumstances, *He* is the one who grows larger.

In Psalm 13, David begins by pouring his heart out to God. "How long, Lord? Will you forget me forever? How long will you hide your face from me?" (v. 1). It could be the beginning of a whine fest, had David continued on that path. But the last line reads, "I will sing the Lord's praise, for he has been good to me" (v. 6). David's whining ended because he changed his focus from himself to God.

If you're feeling a little whiny today and can't seem to get out of your funk, don't fret any longer. Read Psalm 13 and follow David's example of shifting your focus from your circumstances to your God.

Emily

The tablet of your heart

As My son, keep my words and store up my commands within you.
Keep my commands and you will live; guard my teachings
as the apple of your eye. Bind them on your fingers;
write them on the tablet of your heart.
Proverbs 7:1-3 NIV

Your goal should be to live your life in such a way that your actions reflect your time with the Lord. If the only way for others to see that you've spent time in God's Word is by seeing how many journals you have on your shelf, then your time has not been productive.

Others should be able to see Christ in you by how you live, not by how you write about it. Don't get so caught up in writing God's commands on tablets that you neglect to write them on the tablet of your heart.

Emily

Celebrate to honor God

Then celebrate the Festival of Harvest to honor the Lord your God.
Deuteronomy 16:10 NLT

God commanded His people to celebrate several feasts and festivals each year. And although we don't celebrate these same Old Testament feasts and festivals today, I do believe with all of my heart that God still wants His children to celebrate. And what better reason to celebrate than the birth of His Son!

Deuteronomy 16 reveals six instructions for celebrating God's way. By following these same six instructions today, we can celebrate Christmas God's way—in a way that gives Him glory and priority.

The first reason why we celebrate Christmas is simply to honor the Lord. The primary purpose of Christmas isn't shopping and decorating. The primary purpose of Christmas isn't giving and receiving. The primary purpose of Christmas isn't even family and friends. The primary purpose of Christmas is to honor the Lord. So, even as you're shopping, decorating, giving and receiving, make Jesus your primary focus, and you will honor the Lord.

Laurie

Celebrate by giving to God

*Bring him a voluntary offering in proportion to
the blessings you have received from him.*
Deuteronomy 16:10 NLT

The second way to celebrate Christmas God's way is to celebrate by giving to God. Before you give anything to anyone, make your first gift to God. How? By giving to His work through your local church first then to other missions and ministries who honor Him as well. And how much should you give? In proportion to how He has blessed you and as you are able.

Laurie

Celebrate here

*This is a time to celebrate before the Lord your God
at the designated place of worship he will
choose for his name to be honored.*
Deuteronomy 16:11 NLT

Being homesick (or heartsick) during the holidays is hard. You want to go home for Christmas. You want to be with your family and friends. You long to celebrate Christmas like you did in years past. But now, you live here. You can't go home for Christmas. And even if you could, it probably wouldn't be the same. So, what do you do? Settle for a full-blown case of the holiday humbugs?

No, you celebrate Christmas "at the designated place of worship" God has chosen for you. And that's here. In the place where you are right now. You honor the Lord in the place He has chosen for you by celebrating *here*.

Laurie

December 9

Celebrate with others

> *Celebrate with your sons and daughters,*
> *your male and female servants, the Levites from your towns,*
> *and the foreigners, orphans, and widows who live among you.*
> Deuteronomy 16:11 NLT

If family and friends are near, celebrate Christmas with them. But don't forget to include others, especially those who are alone or in need. Prayerfully consider how to include others outside of your family in your Christmas celebration.

These are just a few ideas, but pray about it and the Lord will show you who and how to include others in your Christmas celebration:

- Invite an elderly neighbor to attend Christmas Eve services with you.

- Provide gifts for children who are separated from their parents. For example, *Project Angel Tree* is a beautiful outreach to children who have a parent in prison.

- Many women's shelters welcome gifts for the women and children who live there. Everyday essentials like toothpaste, body wash, shampoo and deodorant are always appreciated as are clothing and gifts for the children.

- Contact a nursing home in your area. Ask how you and your family can bless one of more of their residents who are in need or who will be alone at Christmas.

Even if you're planning to celebrate Christmas with family and friends, don't forget those who are alone and in need—and there are so many.

Laurie

Celebrate by remembering

Remember that you were once slaves in Egypt.
Deuteronomy 16:12 NLT

Unlike the Israelites, you were never enslaved in Egypt. But a slave you once were.

In your B.C. life (before Christ), you were a slave to your own sinful nature (Romans 6). And the truth is, before Christ, you were a slave to Satan himself (Eph. 2:1-3). So one way to celebrate Christmas God's way is to remember: you once were a slave, but Jesus set you free! As you celebrate Christmas—the birth of your Savior and Redeemer—celebrate by remembering.

Laurie

Celebrate with happiness and joy

This festival will be a happy time
of celebrating... a time of great joy for all.
Deuteronomy 16:14-15 NLT

Merry Christmas! It's a simple phrase we should say often and practice religiously. Why? Because when it comes to celebrating, happiness and great joy are on God's to-do list—and that in itself should make you happy.

Christmas perfectionists may get everything on their Christmas to-do lists done, but I'm pretty sure they don't have much fun doing it. So for the next few days, say goodbye to your inner perfectionist. Laugh. Have fun. Play Christmas music. Sing along. Decorate Christmas cookies with your children without saying a single word about the mess. You'll make God (and many others) so happy.

Laurie

Every word

But Jesus told him, "No! The Scriptures say,
'People do not live by bread alone, but by every word
that comes from the mouth of God.'"
Matthew 4:4 NLT

Have you ever read the entire Bible? The Bible is the venue through which God speaks. When you study only parts of the Bible and not the whole thing, you're limiting God's ability to communicate with you efficiently. It's as if you prayed, "God, tell me how to live my life. Tell me how to face my challenges. Tell me what your will is. But, don't use Leviticus, Revelation, or any of the minor prophets to do it."

The Bible is God's love letter to you. Not just the "popular" passages, but the whole thing. He wrote every chapter and every verse for you. Whether it takes you a month or a decade, commit to reading every word. You'll discover how much easier it is to discern His voice when you don't shut His mouth.

Emily

December 13

An omer of manna

Moses said, "This is what the LORD has commanded:
'Take an omer of manna and keep it for the generations to come,
so they can see the bread I gave you to eat in the desert
when I brought you out of Egypt.'"
Exodus 16:32 NIV

Have you ever noticed that sometimes you have to learn the same lessons over and over again? The Israelites were like that. Even though God provided for them in supernatural ways, like by providing manna for them to eat, they still had times when they doubted Him. By commanding the Israelites to take an omer of manna and to preserve it for future generations, He was providing a tangible reminder of His faithfulness.

We've all had times when the Lord has provided for us, but there still seem to be times when we doubt His provisions as well. Why not get an object—a rock, a charm, a piece of art, anything you can think of—to keep as a visual reminder of what God has done for you.

Emily

What if?

> But Joseph said to them, "Don't be afraid. Am I in the place
> of God? You intended to harm me, but God intended it for good
> to accomplish what is now being done, the saving of many lives.
> So then, don't be afraid. I will provide for you and your children."
> And he reassured them and spoke kindly to them.
>
> Genesis 50:19-21 NIV

God is sovereign in all of His ways. He allowed Joseph's brothers to carry out a wicked scheme against him, but He used that wicked scheme to set off a chain reaction that ultimately resulted in good—the salvation of an entire nation.

However, there is an equally important truth that always parallels the sovereignty of God: man has been given a free will. We have the power to choose how we will respond to the seasons of unjust suffering, sorrow, and loss that God sovereignly allows to touch our lives. Joseph resisted bitterness, hatred, unforgiveness, passion, lust and pride and instead chose to react with love, forgiveness, morality and humility.

What if you, too, would accept everything God has sovereignly allowed to touch your life and believe that He has a good purpose in all of it? What if you, too, would choose to steadfastly hold on to your faith and respond in obedience and righteousness in every season of your life? What if?

Laurie

December 15

Thunder

*Unannounced, an angel of God appeared just to the right
of the altar of incense. Zechariah was paralyzed in fear.*
Luke 1:11-12 MSG

Usually, you have a little warning before you hear thunder.
A little rain. Some wind. A flash of lightning, perhaps. But
what about those times when thunder catches you completely
off guard?

I imagine that's what it was like for Elizabeth and her husband,
Zechariah. Because he was a priest, he was used to communicating
with God. But, for the most part, the conversation was pretty
one-sided. Ever since the time of the Old Testament prophets,
God had remained silent.

Until that day in the temple, that is.

Most people think that God broke His long silence when
Gabriel appeared to Mary. But we forget, before Gabriel brought
good news to Mary, Joseph and the shepherds, he spoke to
Zechariah first.

After four hundred years of silence. Four hundred years of
drought. Four hundred years of nothing.

Thunder.

In that single moment, God broke His silence, a childless couple
received the promise of a son, and the groundwork was laid for a
desperate nation to receive its savior.

Thunder, indeed.

Emily

Elizabeth's Thunder

*When Elizabeth heard Mary's greeting, the baby leaped
in her womb, and Elizabeth was filled with the Holy Spirit.
In a loud voice she exclaimed: "Blessed are you among
women, and blessed is the child you will bear!"*
Luke 1:41-42 NIV

As miraculous as Elizabeth's pregnancy was, Mary's pregnancy was even more so. But not once did Elizabeth become jealous or bitter that her moment of thunder was dimmed by Mary's spotlight. Instead, Elizabeth was ecstatic! She saw the bigger picture. She knew that what she and Mary were experiencing wasn't about their miraculous pregnancies at all. It wasn't about who was the most blessed. It wasn't about whose thunder was louder.

It was about the long-awaited Messiah finally coming to earth.

Elizabeth knew that what was happening to her and Mary was happening for the sole purpose of bringing glory to God. And so she praised Him. She didn't compare notes. She didn't accuse God of playing favorites. She didn't belittle her blessing because it wasn't the same as someone else's. Instead, she did what we should all do when we see our fellow sisters being blessed—she praised the One from whom all blessings flow.

And her initial response to Mary's news, I believe, had a direct influence on how their sons' ministries unfolded years later.

Emily

December 17

John's thunder

So John's disciples came to him and said, "Rabbi,
the man you met on the other side of the Jordan River,
the one you identified as the Messiah, is also baptizing people.
And everybody is going to him instead of coming to us."
John 3:26 NLT

Mary stayed with Elizabeth for three months, but after their visit was over, she returned home and they both went their separate ways. Elizabeth gave birth to John. Mary gave birth to Jesus. And the Bible doesn't mention any further encounters between the two women.

It's not until their sons are grown that we see the long-term effects of Elizabeth's thunder-sharing spirit thirty years before.

"Rabbi, the man you met on the other side of the Jordan River, the one you identified as the Messiah, is also baptizing people. And everybody is going to him instead of coming to us." Translation: "John! Jesus is stealing your thunder!"

Can you see how history repeats itself? The comparison, the anger and the jealousy that could have easily surfaced between Elizabeth and Mary decades earlier again had the potential to surface between their sons.

John could have taken the bait. He could have responded with, "Really? Well, how many people has He baptized? More than me? Less? How many disciples does He have? How often does He perform miracles? What is His official stance on locusts and honey?"

But he didn't. Instead, he simply said: "No one can receive anything unless God gives it from heaven. You yourselves know how plainly I told you, 'I am not the Messiah. I am only here to prepare the way for him'" (John 3:27-28 NLT).

Emily

God's thunder

"Therefore, I am filled with joy at his success.
He must become greater and greater,
and I must become less and less."
John 3:29-30 NLT

When was the last time you were filled with joy at the success of someone else? It's kind of hard when we prefer not to share our thunder. But John knew what his mother, Elizabeth, also knew.

It's not really our thunder at all.

The blessings. The miracles. The excitement. They all come from God, and the glory is all His. "God's voice thunders in marvelous ways; he does great things beyond our understanding" (Job 37:5 NIV).

Mary couldn't steal Elizabeth's thunder, because it wasn't hers to begin with.

Jesus couldn't steal John's thunder, because it wasn't his to begin with.

And no one can steal your thunder either, because the thunder is not yours. The glory. The spotlight. The attention. The ticker-tape parade. The thunder.

All God's.

Emily

December 19

There is a season

To every thing there is a season...a time to plant,
and a time to pluck up that which is planted.
Ecclesiastes 3:1-2 KJV

The seasons of our lives often mirror the seasons of nature. When life is joyous and peaceful, when we feel bright and alive, when almost everything in our life seems warm and wonderful, we experience a kind of springtime. When life heats up and we find ourselves seizing new opportunities and responsibilities resulting in a more accelerated way of life, we often experience a kind of summer. When the winds of change begin to blow through our lives leaving us feeling unsteady, uneasy and unsure, we experience a kind of autumn. And when we face prolonged challenges and difficult circumstances, when we feel isolated and alone, when life seems cold and hard, we experience a kind of winter in our lives.

Each season is distinctly different and includes its own unique blessings and challenges.

Laurie

*Now the Passover and the Festival of Unleavened Bread
were only two days away, and the chief priests and the teachers
of the law were scheming to arrest Jesus secretly and kill him.*
Mark 14:1 NIV

It's ironic that the Pharisees were so concerned about celebrating the Passover that they didn't notice that the Passover Lamb—the ultimate sacrifice—was standing right there in front of them. Instead they were distracted by their routines, obligations and traditions. God Himself walked the very streets where they walked, but they were too busy being religious to notice.

Perhaps you're distracted as well.

It would be like turning your back on a starving child because you're late to volunteer at a soup kitchen. Ignoring your husband because you're reading a book about how to improve your marriage. Skipping your quiet time for a whole week because you're too busy with your obligations at church.

Are you missing the relationship because you're distracted by being religious?

Emily

Remarkable things

They were all struck with astonishment and began
glorifying God; and they were filled with fear, saying,
"We have seen remarkable things today."
Luke 5:26 NASB

From His birth, through His childhood, in His ministry and through His miracles, Jesus consistently glorified God every day of His life. Yet, Jesus' greatest glory was witnessed not through His life, but through His death.

The glory of the cross. Think about it. Without the cross there would be no redemption. Without the cross there would be no resurrection. Without the cross we would forever fall short of the glory of God (Rom. 3:23). There's glory in the cross.

One day we, too, will see remarkable things. We will be eyewitnesses of Christ's glory. Imagine what that day is going to be like! But until the trumpet sounds and we meet Him in the air, or until by death we are absent from the body and at home with the Lord, may the glorious results of the cross be visible in our everyday lives as we take up our cross and *glo*!

Laurie

The power of "if"

*If you fully obey the Lord your God and
carefully follow all his commands I give you today,
the Lord your God will set you high above all the nations
on earth. All these blessings will come on you and
accompany you if you obey the Lord your God.*
Deuteronomy 28:1-2 NIV

In the Old Testament, God was always very clear on what would happen if the Israelites obeyed him. If they obeyed, they would be blessed; if they disobeyed, they would be cursed. However, the root of the Israelites' problems was that they failed to understand the power of the word *if*.

God gives us a lot of promises in the Bible, but many of those promises are conditional and depend upon us. *If* you obey God's commands, *then* you will be blessed. God does not go by many formulas, but one formula that I would count on is this: Obedience leads to blessings.

Emily

Need a lift?

*The Lord upholds all those who fall and
lifts up all who are bowed down.*
Psalm 145:14 NIV

It's when the climb is the hardest that we need a lift from our Father the most. But sometimes, in this world that thrives on independence and pride, we never stop to readjust during our obstacles and challenges. If anything, it's when the times are the hardest that our independent, prideful natures kick in and we push ourselves that much more.

It's more difficult to lift someone up when he's moving around than it is to lift him up when he's still. God wants to help us through our times of trouble, but most of the time we never give Him the chance. We're too busy moving, climbing, trying, working and doing it on our own to pause on the landing and readjust.

Are the stairs in front of you high? Is your climb steep? Pause for awhile. Pray. Be still long enough for God to have a chance to lift you up. He promises in His Word that He will.

Emily

Self-abasement

He is so rich in kindness and grace that he purchased
our freedom with the blood of his Son and forgave our sins.
Ephesians 1:7 NLT

There's no way around the fact that we are sinners, unworthy and undeserving of God's grace and forgiveness. However, when we tilt the truth too much in the direction of our unworthiness, we fall into the sin of self-abasement, or condemnation. God convicts; He does not condemn. So when we choose to beat ourselves up over our past mistakes and past sins, constantly bemoaning, "I'm not worthy," to our reflections in the mirror, it renders us paralyzed for the kingdom of God.

It may sound spiritual to acknowledge your unworthiness, but focusing on it is the opposite of faith because it is the unbelief in God's ability to forgive.

Laurie

Wonderfully made

For you created my inmost being;
you knit me together in my mother's womb.
I praise you because I am fearfully and wonderfully made.
Psalm 139:13-14 NIV

Before my husband and I had our first child, we painted these words from Psalm 139 on the wall of the nursery. Since then, each of our four children has spent hundreds of nights sleeping under this poetic reminder from God's Word. It's the perfect declaration for a new soul entering this uncertain world for the first time.

But might I suggest that it is also the perfect declaration for the old soul who is struggling in this uncertain world for the umpteenth time. This verse that seems so fitting hanging above the bed of a newborn is just as fitting to hang above your own bed. Perhaps you need to paint Psalm 139 on the wall of your heart. Perhaps you need to be reminded that He created your inmost being, wonderfully and perfectly according to His divine specifications. No mistakes. No errors. No duplicates. You are who you are because He made you *you.*

Emily

Teach me your paths

Show me your ways, Lord, teach me your paths.
Psalm 25:4 NIV

I remember the first time I took my boys on a walk around the block. When we left the house, they could sense that we were walking away from home and expected that there would come a point that we needed to stop and turn around in order to make it back home. But we kept walking forward instead. Suddenly, our house was right in front of us again and they were so confused as to how we got there when it felt like we were walking away the whole time. They didn't understand that we were walking in a circle.

Sometimes it may feel like every step you take is leading you farther and farther away from where you believe the Lord is leading you. But when He directs your paths, it might be that home is just around the corner.

Emily

Not struggling along

*This High Priest of ours understands our weaknesses,
for he faced all of the same testings we do, yet he did not sin.*
Hebrews 4:15 NLT

You are never alone in your struggles. Sometimes you feel alone, don't you? Sometimes you feel that everyone else has it all together and you keep struggling with the same old things. You feel like a failure. Girl, listen. You are not alone. You're struggling. I'm struggling, and the Bible says that you and I are to bear one another's burdens and to confess our sins to one another and to pray for each other.

Don't think that what you're going through is something no one else has faced. We've all faced these things. Jesus, your High Priest, understands your struggles, and you have brothers and sisters in Christ who understand as well—friends who want to help you and encourage you through your struggle.

Laurie

Gospel of peace

*Stand firm then… with your feet fitted with the readiness
that comes from the gospel of peace.*
Ephesians 6:14-15 NIV

It is important to note that when Paul tells us to put on the armor of God, he tells us to have our feet fitted with the "gospel of peace," not with just "peace." There's a significant difference between the world's view of peace and the "gospel of peace," which is the biblical view of peace.

• Worldly peace strives for complete unity by sacrificing convictions.

• Worldly peace strives for compromise at all cost.

• Worldly peace strives for tolerance more than it cries for holiness.

• Worldly peace strives for a world with absolutely no conflict at all.

The difference between the two views of peace is that only the Gospel of peace takes into consideration one thing—the Cross. And when we are at peace with God through the Cross, we are automatically at war with Satan and the world.

Emily

Your unique way

So David triumphed over the Philistine with a
sling and a stone; without a sword in his hand
he struck down the Philistine and killed him.

1 Samuel 17:50 NIV

Just before David's battle with Goliath, Saul took his own sword, armor and helmet and clothed David with them. But David wasn't comfortable walking around in Saul's armor and being weighed down by Saul's weapons, so he gave everything back and chose to fight the giant in his own way instead.

David knew that he would not be successful if he tried to copy someone else at the expense of his own unique style. Successful leadership begins by embracing the qualities that God has given you and resisting the urge to become someone else's clone.

When someone comes along with qualities you find admirable, use their example to enhance your own unique way, not to abandon it.

Laurie

He accepts your prayer

Away from me, all you who do evil,
for the Lord has heard my weeping.
The Lord has heard my cry for mercy;
the Lord accepts my prayer.
Psalm 6:8 NIV

Sometimes my mind is so full of accusations and lies that I cannot find the truth on my own. If I try to fight bad thoughts with good thoughts, I feel as if I'm attacking a forest of thorns with a rubber machete. It's pointless. I might as well give up and give in. But, when I fight bad thoughts with God's thoughts, it's as if the forest of thorns just melts away and I can see the truth once again.

Even when you repent of your sin and ask God to forgive you, Satan will keep trying to condemn you with it over and over again. But the truth is that the Lord has heard your weeping. He hears you when you cry for mercy. He listens. He forgives. And He accepts your prayer.

Emily

Glowing

> When Moses came down Mount Sinai carrying the
> two stone tablets inscribed with the terms of the covenant,
> he wasn't aware that his face had become radiant because
> he had spoken to the Lord…. But whenever he went into the
> Tent of Meeting to speak with the Lord, he would remove the
> veil until he came out again. Then he would give the people
> whatever instructions the Lord had given him, and the
> people of Israel would see the radiant glow of his face.
> Exodus 34:29, 34-35 NLT

When Moses descended from Mount Sinai after meeting with God for forty days, the evidence of his encounter was written upon his face. God's glory visibly shone from Moses' countenance.

We may not literally glow as Moses did, but the glory that God has given us is even better than the glory the children of Israel saw upon Moses' face because our lives can visibly reflect and reveal the glory of the One who inhabits us. Psalm 26:8 says, "Lord, I love the house where you live, the place where your glory dwells" (NIV). When you are inhabited by God, His glory dwells is in *you*. Are you *glo*-ing?

Laurie

Resources

Notes

January 24

[1] John F. Walvoord and Roy B. Zuck, *The Bible Knowledge Commentary,* (Wheaton, IL: Victor Books, 1984), 468.

January 24

[2] Spiros Zodhiates, *The Complete Word Study Dictionary New Testament,* (Chattanooga, TN: AMG Publishers, Revised edition 1993), 1280.

January 29

[3] Spiros Zodhiates, *The Complete Word Study Dictionary New Testament,* (Chattanooga, TN: AMG Publishers, Revised edition 1993), 1295.

February 12

[4] Warren Baker, *The Complete Word Study Dictionary Old Testament,* Chattanooga, TN: AMG Publishers, 2003), 354.

February 14

[5] Warren Baker, *The Complete Word Study Dictionary Old Testament,* Chattanooga, TN: AMG Publishers, 2003), 2371.

April 19

[6] Herbert Lockyer, Sr., ed., *Nelson's Illustrated Bible Dictionary* (Nashville: Thomas Nelson Publishers, 1986), 1077.

May 28

[7] Emily E. Ryan, *Who Has Your Heart: The Single Woman's Pursuit of Godliness* (Grand Rapids: Discovery House Publishers, 2006), 72-73.

August 4

[8] Spiros Zodhiates, *The Complete Word Study Dictionary New Testament,* (Chattanooga, TN: AMG Publishers, Revised edition 1993), 62.

[9] Ibid, p. 1031.

[10] Ibid, p. 1469.

September 8

[11] John F. Walvoord and Roy B. Zuck, *The Bible Knowledge Commentary,* (Wheaton, IL: Victor Books, 1984), 624.

About Priority Ministries

When your relationship with God comes first in your life, everything else falls into place.

Because it's as simple, and as difficult, as that, we're here to help you make God your #1 priority.

Priority Ministries was founded by Laurie Cole in 2003 to encourage and equip women to give God glory and priority in their everyday lives. We do this by producing and providing practical, biblical, female-friendly Bible studies and books, and by teaching and proclaiming God's Word at women's events, conferences, and on our Glo Girl Blog.

Priority Ministries is a non-profit 501(c)3 organization and operates on a debt-free basis, so every penny of your tax-deductible donation is used for ministry.

To inquire about having Laurie or Emily speak at your event, to preview our resources, or to support Priority with your financial gift, visit us online at **priorityministries.com**.

Priority Ministries
Encouraging Women to Give God Glory & Priority

Priority Ministries
711 West Bay Area Blvd., Suite 214
Webster, TX 77598
832.632.2197
866.968.4564 (toll-free)

For further reading

All of the readings found in *Glo: 365 Devotions to Give God Priority* were compiled, edited and repurposed from these resources:

Beauty by The Book: Becoming a Biblically Beautiful Woman

True beauty isn't found in magazines, cosmetics counters, or at the gym. It's found in the pages of Proverbs with women who model what to do, and what not to do, in order to be beautiful at any age.

7 weeks • workbook/video study • Free videos available online

Beauty by The Book for Teens: Becoming a Biblically Beautiful Young Woman

Is it possible to be beautiful without short shorts, cleavage, excessive flirting, or the perfect body? The world may say no, but the book of Proverbs says yes! Discover the truth about beauty now, and avoid a lifetime of regret later.

7 weeks • workbook/video study • Free videos available online

There is a Season: Experiencing Contentment in Every Season of Life

In every season and circumstance, you can still find joy, purpose, and meaning. Even when you think it's out of reach, God offers contentment and divine rest. By understanding the seasons of your life, you can learn to thrive in them.

11 weeks • workbook/video study

The Temple: Glorifying God in Your Everyday Life

Even in everyday, mundane tasks, you have the supernatural ability to *glo* – glorify God – because you are His temple. Discover how to shine and fulfill God's greatest purpose for your life. You *glo* girl!

11 weeks • workbook/video study

Guilt-Free Quiet Times: Exposing the Top Ten Myths about Your Time with God

When it comes to your quiet time, it's time to say no to someone else's rules or magic formulas that work perfectly for him or her but only create chaos and guilt in your own life. With the perfect blend of sarcasm and Scripture, Emily Ryan exposes the most common myths about traditional quiet times and gives you the freedom you need to chase after God in your own unique way.

118 pages • small group discussion questions

Who Has Your Heart? The Single Woman's Pursuit of Godliness

When your "urge to merge" begins to surge and you're tired of studying all of the married women of the Bible, turn to the unnamed, unmarried and unshakable biblical heroine from Judges 11 - Jephthah's daughter. You'll discover ten aspects of her character that are essential for every woman, single or not, to emulate, and quickly appreciate why Jephthah's daughter is the scriptural role model you have been waiting to discover.

238 pages • small group discussion questions

We're busy just like you. So this blog is dedicated to busy women everywhere who may have a million things going on, but still want to make God the #1 thing. It can be done, and we offer guilt-free teaching and resources to help you do it. You can *glo*, even in your busy life!

www.priorityministries.com/christian-womens-blog

www.priorityministries.com/shop

Available in 2015
from Priority Ministries

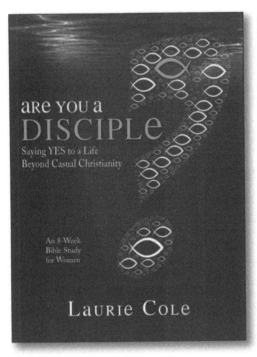

Are You a DISCIPLE? Saying YES to a Life Beyond Casual Christianity

8 weeks • workbook/video study

Warrior Princess: Join the Battle

4 sessions • video study